PSYCHOLOGICAL STRESS IN THE CAMPUS COMMUNITY

Theory, Research, and Action

Community Psychology Series, Volume 3
American Psychological Association, Division 27

THE COMMUNITY PSYCHOLOGY SERIES
SPONSORED BY
DIVISION 27 OF THE AMERICAN PSYCHOLOGICAL ASSOCIATION
SERIES EDITOR, DANIEL ADELSON, PH.D.

The Community Psychology Series has as its central purpose the building of philosophic, theoretical, scientific and empirical foundations for action research in the community and in its subsystems, and for education and training for such action research.

As a publication of the Division of Community Psychology, the series is particularly concerned with the development of community psychology as a sub-area of psychology. In general, it emphasizes the application and integration of theories and findings from other areas of psychology, and in particular the development of community psychology methods, theories, and principles, as these stem from actual community research and practice.

TITLES IN THE COMMUNITY PSYCHOLOGY SERIES

PSYCHOLOGICAL STRESS
IN THE CAMPUS COMMUNITY

Theory, Research, and Action

Community Psychology Series, Volume 3
American Psychological Association, Division 27

Edited by

Bernard L. Bloom
University of Colorado, Boulder

Daniel Adelson, Series Editor
University of California, San Francisco

Behavioral Publications, Inc.
New York

Library of Congress Catalog Number 74–6184
ISBN: 0–87705–145–3
Copyright © 1975 by Behavioral Publications, Inc.

BEHAVIORAL PUBLICATIONS, Inc.
72 Fifth Avenue
New York, New York 10011

Printed in the United States of America
56789   987654321

Library of Congress Cataloging in Publication Data

Bloom, Bernard L
  Psychological stress in the campus community.

  (Community psychology series, issue 3)
  1. College students—Psychology. I. Title. II. Series. [DNLM: 1. Stress, Psychological. 2. Students. 3. Universities. W1CO429W no. 3 1974/ WA352 P974 1974]
LB3609.B62   378.1'98'1   74–6184

Contributors

JAMES H. BANNING is currently Dean of Student Affairs, University of Missouri, Columbia, and was formerly the director of the project "Improving Mental Health Services on Western Campuses" based at the Western Interstate Commission for Higher Education in Boulder, Colorado. Prior to coming to WICHE he served as the director of the University of Colorado Counseling and Testing Department. He began campus mental health work as a clinical psychologist but has found his interests moving from the concepts of service and remediation to the concepts of prevention and enhancement. Along with this change, his interest in intervention strategies has also changed in focus from the individual to the institution. Viewing the campus as a community is exciting and useful to him in his efforts to bring about changes in higher education that will benefit the growth and development of students and their institutions.

BERNARD L. BLOOM is currently in the Psychology Department at the University of Colorado. After a decade as a practicing clinical psychologist, he entered the field of community mental health by spending a year with Gerald Caplan and his staff at Harvard School of Public Health and then serving for three years as a mental health consultant with the National Institute of Mental Health. He has been at the University of Colorado since 1965 and

5

his interest in applying community mental health concepts to the campus community began shortly thereafter.

TOM CARSKADON entered Oberlin College in 1965. He says jokingly that this is where he first became interested in preventive aspects of college student mental health programs since the seemingly endless array of crises, problems, dilemmas, and predicaments that students there seemed to get into just couldn't *all* have been necessary! Tom majored in psychology under Dr. Ralph Turner and entered the clinical psychology program at the University of Colorado in 1968. He continued his interests in teaching and in college student mental health programs, and the present article is part of his dissertation research under Dr. Bloom. Tom is interning this year at the University of Florida, after which he hopes to find a job teaching and working on college student programs.

CARL CLARKE received his Ph.D. at the University of Florida in 1965 after earlier education at Atlanta Christian College and the University of Hawaii. His major interests are in psychotherapy, community mental health, and marriage and the family. He is currently the director of the Marriage and College Life Project at the University of Florida Student Mental Health Program.

PATRICK E. COOK, Associate Professor of Psychology, the Florida State University, received his B.A. from the University of Rochester and his Ph.D. from the University of Texas at Austin. While at the University of Texas he was one of the first participants in the Community Mental Health program and he blames his interest in community psychology on Ira Iscoe, the director of that program. He previously was an intern, then Staff Psychologist at South Shore Mental Health Center in Massachusetts. He is the editor of *Community Psychology and Community Mental Health: Introductory Readings.*

ROBERT DEBRÉ, now retired, was formerly the Director of the Institute of Hygiene and Bacteriology in Strasbourg, and subsequently Professor of Medicine and Director of the Children's Hospital in Paris.

DAVID FALK received his Ph.D. from Northwestern University. He has worked in a variety of mental health settings in Illinois and Colorado and, while in Colorado, served as a consultant and task force member for the Western Interstate Commission for Higher Education project directed by Dr. Banning and as a consultant on youth-initiated projects for the Mental Health Services Development Branch of the National Institute of Mental Health. He is now Chief of the Evaluation Division, Pennsylvania Governor's Council on Drug and Alcohol Abuse.

BEN C. FINNEY worked for ten years as Chief for Psychotherapy in the Psychology Service after completing the clinical psychology training program at Berkeley in 1951. Training young clinicians and conducting group therapy sessions with them and other hospital staff taught him that it is not just the "sick" person who can benefit from group therapy, especially when people are working together. When he moved to San Jose State College in 1961, on a split appointment between the Psychology Department and the Counseling Center, he was disturbed by the isolation among the students and the extent to which this isolation seemed to be fostered by the environment. The Peer Program grew out of his efforts to meet affiliative needs of the students. As a professor, he found that he could have multiple relationships with students—as professor, therapist, and friend—and that the more he shared himself with them as a person, the more they gave him back in affection and respect. He has developed a number of different therapy techniques and has found that therapy is not the "special and circumscribed" relationship that he was taught. A wide variety of ways of dealing with clients can be tried, as long as the client and the therapist approach it in a sense of mutual exploration.

SEYMOUR L. HALLECK has recently joined the Department of Psychiatry at the University of North Carolina after having been at the University of Wisconsin for fourteen years. During his association with the University of Wisconsin he was the director of Student Health Psychiatry and has been active as an interpreter of the issues concerning university students during the turbulent years of campus unrest. He is the author of numerous publications dealing with the student in the university community and most recently authored *The Politics of Therapy*, published by Science House in 1971.

JOHN HINKLE is Mental Health Coordinator at the Colorado State University Student Health Center. Previously, he worked for five years at the Colorado State University Counseling Center where he helped develop married student programs on the campus. A married clinical psychologist with four children, his interest in marriage programs grew out of his work with couples and families in community mental health centers. His own parenting experiences contribute to recognition of the need for preventive growth-inducing programs for people.

JOHN KALAFAT is an Assistant Professor in the Psychology Department and Counseling Center at the Florida State University. He received his Ph.D. in clinical psychology from the University of Colorado in 1970. His predoctoral professional experience included a year of work as a research assistant at Fels Institute, and an internship at Camarillo State Hospital. In his present position, one of his major commitments has been serving as one of the two coordinators of the Telephone Counseling Service. He has also served as Coordinator of Outreach Programs for the Counseling Center.

JOSEPH KATZ is Director of Research for Human Development and Educational Policy and Professor of Human Development at the State University of New York at Stony Brook. Before coming to Stony Brook he was Executive Director of the Institute for the Study of Human Problems at Stanford University. At the Human Problems Institute he directed the Student Development Study in which the 1961 entrants at Berkeley and at Stanford were followed through their four college years by means of interviews, personality inventories, questionnaires, and other instruments. His interests have centered on studying development from age seventeen onward, with particular attention to the implications of personality theory for educational practice. He has worked as a clinician for several years and has a special fondness for applying the clinical point of view to the study of nonpatient populations. Recently he has carried his developmental studies into the post-college phase and has been particularly interested in the development of adult women. Among the books he has coauthored are *The American College* (1962), *No Time for Youth* (1968), and *Services for Students* (1973).

MARV MOORE, Associate Professor in the Department of Psychology at Colorado State University is currently the Associate Director of the Colorado State University Counseling Center. He is responsible for married student programs and during the past four years has developed a variety of marriage training workshops.

WESTON H. MORRILL is Associate Professor of Psychology at Colorado State University and director of a project funded by the National Institute of Mental Health to study outreach programs in college counseling. He has been director of the University Counseling Center and the Office of Student Development at Colorado State University. Previously, 1965–66, he was Assistant Professor of Education at Michigan State University. He was awarded the Ph.D. in Counseling Psychology in 1966 from the University of Missouri at Columbia.

SAMUEL PEARLMAN is presently on the faculty of Brooklyn College of the City University of New York, with a background of service in the area of college mental health that goes back nearly a third of a century. It is an area of psychological application which has kept him young and his heart is sometimes saddened in the contemplation of his peers who cannot see the personal satisfactions of a professional commitment to young people in university settings. He has published a number of articles on the subject of college mental health, the latest among them focusing on drug usage on the campus. His latest book (1970) gives evidence of a widening horizon: *University Mental Health—In-*

ternational Perspectives. During this past decade, he has served as President of the New York State Psychological Association, of the New York Society of Clinical Psychologists, and of the American Association of State Psychology Boards. He has also served on the American Psychological Association Council of Representatives as well as on the Committee on Scientific and Professional Ethics and Conduct. He is currently the chairman of the New York State Board for Psychology, and the Regional Director of the American Board for Professional Psychology.

NEVITT SANFORD is currently the Scientific Director of the Wright Institute in Berkeley and for a number of years has been concerned in his writings with issues in the growth and development of young people living and learning in college settings. He is a member of the San Francisco Psychoanalytic Society and has been honored with the Kurt Lewin Memorial Award of the Society for the Psychological Study of Social Issues in 1969 and with the award for Distinguished Contribution to Clinical Psychology in 1970. He edited *The American College: A Psychological and Social Interpretation of Higher Learning,* one of the most influential volumes in this field in recent years.

FRANK R. TIMMONS is currently a post-doctoral fellow at the Menninger Foundation. While he and his wife were serving as Peace Corps Volunteers in Turkey, he became interested in discontent among volunteers and their subsequent early return to the United States. After completing his tenure in Turkey and entering the program in clinical psychology at the University of Colorado he was struck by how much alienation and withdrawal among college students seemed to resemble what he had observed among volunteers. This interest then became the focus of much of his study while at the University of Colorado. Along with his professional interests, his wife, Karen, a psychiatric social worker, and their son, Jeffrey, are his major sources of satisfaction and joy in his life.

MARY TYLER is an assistant professor in the Psychology Department and Counseling Center at Florida State University. She received her Ph.D. in clinical psychology from the University of Texas at Austin in 1970, after completing an internship at Duke University Medical Center. During her first two years at Florida State University, serving as one of the two coordinators of the Telephone Counseling Service was a major focus of her professional activity. She is currently involved in the development of courses on the psychology of women and in outreach programs aimed at facilitating the personal growth of women students.

THOMAS L. WINDHAM, born in 1944 in Harlem Hospital, New York City, is currently a graduate student in the social psychology program at the University of Colorado. He is working at the Eastside Neighborhood Health Center in Denver as a community psychologist and is teaching a course for the Black Studies Program at the University of Colorado entitled "Culture, Racism, and Alienation." He has taught full-time at Nebraska Wesleyan University and part-time at the extension division of the University of Nebraska. His paper is based upon his own experiences as a Black faculty member and as a Black student at the University of Colorado, New Mexico Highlands University, and the University of Wyoming.

Contents

III.   PROGRAMS IN ACTION

IV.   EPILOGUE

Preface

It is, as my dear Aunt Rose used to say, looking up at the lights in the tall apartments that lined Fifth Avenue in New York City, "a world full of little worlds." And of these worlds perhaps that which has been seen as most like an "ivory tower" is the university campus. And yet herein lies a paradox, for in our times students in their ivory towers have been those in sharpest revolt against major social ills—war, poverty, and dictatorship. A seeming handful by comparison with the larger non-campus world, through strikes, protests, marches, have brought down mighty regimes. Their major weapons—the democratic ethic, morality, common humanity, beyond *status quo* and constraining reinforcements but for freedom and dignity. If it is a world full of little worlds, they are indeed interrelated worlds, and students in the United States and in South America, and in France and Greece seem to be aware of this. Their vision, if less experienced, at times seems clearer. For them, no man is an island. They know for whom the bell tolls.

But each ivory tower is a world of its own, with different values making more or less of a fit for different students —providing conditions that are more or less congenial for its faculty and students—some on the whole fostering growth and others inducing the same alienation and stresses that are felt in the world at large.

In this volume, Bernard L. Bloom has invited a group of contributors to address themselves to the question of stress in the campus community from a number of vantage points, including a review of that special period, late

15

adolescence, which is marked by idealism and also criticism of the adult world especially as represented by parents. In a final section he engages three of the contributors in a conversation that ends on an unfinished issue, almost open-ended, implicitly inviting the reader to join in the discussion around the issue of teacher-student relationships. This conversational form symbolizes perhaps more than the content does what the new thrusts are —an increasing give and take that must at times bring stress not only to students but also to faculty—but certainly also moments of insight, sharing, and joy.

Daniel Adelson
Series Editor

Prologue

Few social institutions are undergoing a more rapid or more significant period of review and renewal than the American university. There is hardly a single aspect of the university that is not the subject of growing critical examination. Not only is the role of the university in the greater society being reviewed, but its fundamental mission, governance policies, and academic philosophy are all undergoing major reconsideration.

It is entirely appropriate and perhaps essential that the university take leadership in its continuing self-examination. All too often, the university has found itself reacting defensively to external criticism, having to deploy vast resources in program or policy justification, in crisis management, and in after-the-fact program modification. What seems most unfortunate is that this state of chronic crisis has made it even more difficult to plan academic and nonacademic university programs in a rational manner. In a way, we have become the victims of our own decisions about resource allocation. We have all been so busy that anticipatory planning has had low priority. Because we have done so little self-study, because we in fact have known so little about the constituencies we serve, crises have developed on many campuses, necessitating the redistribution of our resources to meet these crises. And because of this additional demand on our resources, it has become even more difficult to plan for our universities' futures.

Complicating this problem has been the mounting evidence of great disjunctions in educational philosophy.

17

Students have changed dramatically in the past twenty years and there is no evidence to suggest that the rate of change is decreasing although the direction of change is much more difficult to discern. It certainly comes as no surprise to anyone who lives and works in a university community that students, faculty, and administration differ in very substantial ways in their orientations toward the role of higher education in our society, in their orientation toward the work ethic, in their beliefs as to effective strategies of education, and in many aspects of what might be called "life style."

All these problems take on even greater urgency when we realize that there are now eight million college students, there may soon be ten million young people attending colleges and universities in the United States, and that serious efforts will undoubtedly be continued to eliminate the historical relationships between college attendance on the one hand, and race, ethnic group, and family income on the other hand.

Our college students are a national treasure of incalculable worth and yet it is a fact that we know almost nothing about them. Universities have the opportunity to create growth-inducing climates of unparalleled importance in the lives of young people, not only for the honorable tasks of pursuing and disseminating knowledge but also for assisting students' development and maturation as responsible participating members of the larger community. But our lack of knowledge is one of the constraints limiting our abilities to be helpful. The college years represent times of unprecedented growth and development for young people. Not only is the university the locus of education and training for an increasing proportion of our youth, but the personal experiences in college form the basis for the maturation of life-long values and orientations to the greater society. The experiences of students on college campuses have a major impact on their subsequent lives and help prepare them for significant roles as leaders of the future. It is, therefore, not only for the benefit of the university and the student but also for the ultimate benefit of our entire society that universities should devote some of their resources to the on-going study of their students and the nature of their university experiences. As a consequence of such study, the university can work toward the creation of those kinds of environments which will have an increasingly positive effect on both the personal as well as the intellectual life of the student.

A student brings with him a set of ego demands and resources to help him in making an effective adaptation to the university community. At the university, he finds a complex social system with its own demands and resources. Demands imposed by the social system can come into conflict with the goals internalized by students, while social system resources (including the formal caretaking network) can serve to support the student at those times when his adaptation is threatened. Thus, adaptation to the university is a complex and unstable process, involving both personal and social demands in dynamic, ever-changing interrelationship. At some moments, the adaptation has to be autoplastic, in which the student changes to meet social system demands. At other times the adaptation should be alloplastic, in which changes are induced in the social system to better meet needs of the student. Psychological characteristics of the student and sociological characteristics of the campus are hence in a complementary relationship with each other, a relationship that is always in a state of change. The general trend in American universities, certainly, is for fewer and fewer constraints to be imposed by the social system. Yet this very trend results in more demands being made on the student's inner resources. A campus, responsive to this state of affairs, must organize its formal caretaking network so that students can find sources of support when their inner resources are inadequate. These formal social support systems must be organized in a way that does justice to the student's striving for mastery over his environment.

The contents of this volume reflect the concerns and conceptual framework developed in the preceding paragraphs. The initial section includes three theoretical papers, the first dealing with the university as a stress-inducing system, the second dealing with the psychodynamics of the college student, and the third concerning the role of biological factors in student unrest, and an essay on the Black student on the college campus. The three research reviews, which comprise the second section of this volume, include papers on the college drop out, the assessment of student help-seeking behavior, and a brief overview of college mental health activities outside the United States and Canada. The third section includes a series of brief reports and commentaries on a variety of innovative action programs in selected universities and university-related agencies in the United States. The volume concludes with an edited transcript of a conversation held on April 22, 1972 with three distinguished scholars whose work has been closely identified with the American university.

It is a pleasure to be able to take this opportunity to thank all of the participants involved in this volume for their willingness to prepare the papers that you are about to read. While I have found the editorial role a stimulating one and have enjoyed the editorial responsibilities, the strengths of the volume are in greatest measure a function of the works of the contributing authors.

Bernard L. Bloom

PSYCHOLOGICAL STRESS
IN THE CAMPUS COMMUNITY

Part I

THEORY AND COMMENTARY

1. Campus Environments, Student Stress, and Campus Planning

DAVID FALK

The past several years may well be remembered as a period of great conflict and confrontation on the college and university campus. While the present period has been described as a time of reassessment and calm, the college campus continues to be the setting in which large numbers of students come to experience significant stresses. That the campus should be a stress setting is partly a function of the values, practices, and pressures incorporated into higher education and a function of the unique set of developmental tasks that late adolescents need to master in their movement into adult roles.

The aim of this paper is to review a number of conceptualizations that can be integrated into an analysis of student stress. Such an analysis would reflect the contribution that both individual characteristics and environmental characteristics have in determining outcomes for individuals within institutions of higher education.

The author would like to acknowledge the assistance of Bernard Bloom, Department of Psychology, University of Colorado, Richard Harpel, Office for Student Relations, University of Colorado, and James Banning, Western Interstate Commission for Higher Education, in developing this paper.

Lewin (1951) has asserted that behavior is a function of personality and environment, and Murray (1938) has developed a theoretical position that describes individual behavior in terms of individual needs and environmental press. Environments, according to Murray, can either gratify or frustrate individual needs. Both of these personality theories have clearly focused on the interaction of individuals and environments. Relating these and similar concepts to the college setting, one could say that the college environment represents a complex set of demands, options, and values. This configuration of demands and options interacts with the diverse characteristics and differing developmental stages of the student population. Murray has indicated that an individual would interact with the environment according to the extent that the environment gratifies or frustrates his needs. Pervin (1968) suggests that "individuals are positively attracted toward objects in the environment that hold promise for taking them toward their ideal selves and are negatively disposed toward objects that hold promise for taking them away from their ideal selves [p. 63]." Concepts such as these would lead one to expect that college students are involved in a continuing process of exploration and adjustment with respect to their college environment.

It can also be said the colleges differ from one another with respect to the specific configuration of demands and options they present to students. This may mean that on certain campuses some behaviors will be rewarded while on other campuses the same behaviors may be met with a far different response. Kelly (1970) in his systems analysis of high schools has noted the interdependent nature of social settings and individual coping behaviors. Implicit in such analysis is the notion that there are identifiable behaviors in a given social setting that will produce an optimum level of rewards or need gratifications.

Given the diversity among students and the increasing size and complexity of the university campus, it is likely that many students are far from discovering the optimum conditions for themselves on their campuses. Likewise, there are students who, understanding the options available in the campus environment, find them to be incongruent with personal needs and goals. Still other students come to the university setting with personal problems that are sufficiently severe as to limit their effectiveness in exploring and adjusting to the environment. Such situations, where there is a lack of fit between the needs and goals of the students and the demands and values of the college, constitute such a frequent occurrence as to make them a persistent part of the educational process which cannot be ignored if educational and developmental goals of higher education are to be attained. Stress is seen as the consequence of an inadequate fit of student needs and goals with the college environment. Students experiencing high levels of stress and frustration in their interactions with the college environment are likely to initiate attempts to reduce this negative experience. Such a student may choose from a number of general adjustment strategies including attempts to change himself, change the negative aspects of the environment, or leave the environment.

This discussion suggests a number of possible research areas that could have important implications for those interested in student development, student supportive services, and college environmental planning. What follows is first, a review of a range of research findings on students and on college environments that employ the interactional focus discussed above. Second, a brief review of some attempts to assess college environments and their impact on student perceptions and behavior will be made along with some discussion of recent efforts to develop a planning strategy for college environments. This last issue, a discussion of planning attempts, has great relevance here since such attempts extend research findings based on the interactional model into areas of

policy planning. The aim of planning is to produce congenial and responsive growth-inducing environments for a
wide range of students and thereby reduce the kinds of
stresses and conflicts associated with a poor student-environment fit.

The many research efforts on the college dropout have
very often provided important insights into the interactional nature of student characteristics and educational
environments. In fact, Pervin (1967a) has argued that interactional studies of the college dropout have greater
explanatory power than studies that consider either student characteristics or character of the college environments exclusively. Hirsch and Keniston (1970) state that
the interactional nature of personality characteristics and
college environments helps to explain why findings on the
psychological characteristics of students who withdraw
from college have differed so much from one college to
another.

As a result of their research on dropouts from Yale University, Hirsch and Keniston (1970) state "the act of dropping out seems basically related to the incongruence
between the student's own developmental timetable and
the normative timetable of demands and opportunities of
the college setting at each point in the student's career
[p. 15]." While Hirsch and Keniston were able to find only
a few shared personal characteristics of dropouts, dropouts shared the view that their own diverse developmental needs and goals could not be adequately fulfilled in the
college environment. In describing the college environment Hirsch and Keniston note that "colleges make implicit assumptions about the timing of the intellectual and
psychological development of their students and these
assumptions are embodied in the class-graded demands of
college's informal culture. The college that confronts a
senior is often extremely different in the psychological
meanings and demands from the college that confronts a
freshman in the same institution at the same time. And

students who respond successfully to one set of class-graded college demands may not be as successful with later college pressures [p. 16]." Thus according to Hirsch and Keniston, changing college demands must be matched by new developmental accomplishment on the part of the student. Students who find themselves either behind or ahead of "schedule" in relation to the timetable of environmental demands are subjected to psychological stress. The dropouts in the Hirsch and Keniston study chose neither to transform themselves so as to cope with conflict or to transform the environment so as to make it less stressful. Rather, dropouts chose to increase the distance between themselves and the source of stress—the college environment. Different college environments reinforce some behaviors while discouraging others (Snyder, 1963). Thus, the choice of adaptive strategies is likely to vary according to personality characteristics and environmental features that may influence the effectiveness and rewards for certain adaptive roles. Some further discussion of student adaptive roles related to value conflict has been made by Leininger (1971). She has articulated three adaptive patterns students have employed in the face of stress and value conflict. These include: Type I, active protest and rebellious behaviors; Type II, withdrawn, narcissistic, alienated behavior; and Type III, marked fear behavior. While paralleling the Hirsch and Keniston discussion, Leininger's typology adds what she feels has been the largest campus group—Type III. These are students characterized neither by active protest or withdrawal, but rather an almost ritualistic response to conflict and stress. These students choose to busy themselves with academic studies. What is important here is that general adaptive patterns have been articulated in response to observations of stress conditions on campus.

Pervin (1966), in his work on college dropouts, has found that "a student is likely to withdraw if he finds that his college environment threatens his identity, offers few acceptable solutions to his conflicts and makes unacceptable a period of delay before solution. While in some cases · emphasis upon grievances against the college represents an attempt at externalization of essentially internal conflicts, there are cases in which the personality of the student is ill suited to the atmosphere of the college [p. 160]." Pervin further states that "at another college the student would be left with the same conflicts, but at least they would not be exacerbated, and he would find support for acceptable attempts at solutions [p. 160]."

Pervin and Rubin (1967) found that a discrepancy between self-image and image of the college predicts intention to drop out. Further, Pervin (1966) has found that a discrepancy between self-image and image of the college is associated with dissatisfaction with the college. Similarly, Shaw (1968) has found that students are able to absorb much of the shock of finding their expectations of a certain part of the college environment not met, but when most of the environment is inconsistent with expectations, then the student is more likely to withdraw from that environment.

The above studies, while giving strong support to an interactional stress model of student characteristics and environmental features, focus essentially on the consequences of a "mismatch." In other words, much of the above has focused on the victims of stress without clear specifications of environmental features and processes that increase or decrease stress for diverse student subgroups, and without showing what student characteristics are more associated with susceptibility to specific stresses. Clearly, if one is to deal seriously with the complex problems of the student-environmental fit, more systematic and quantitative efforts will be needed to articulate the dynamics of student-environmental interactions. Such increased specification of the processes involved will greatly extend our current knowledge in preventing dysfunctional stress situations on the college campus.

ASSESSMENTS OF STUDENT-ENVIRONMENT INTERACTION

Numerous research efforts over the past few years have focused on the development of concepts and instruments by which the university environment might be assessed. Of these, the studies by Astin (1968), Pace and Stern (1958), Pace (1963, 1969), Stern (1962a, 1962b), and Pervin (1967a, 1967b, 1968) are most notable. (For a recent review of the environmental assessment literature with some reference to methodological issues see Feldman, 1971.) The instruments developed in the above studies have been devised to suit particular research interests and conceptual schemes: the choice of the preferred method will be dependent on the specific aims of the researcher. There has been some discussion, however, of the benefits of using multiple measures in assessing college environments since the various instruments that have been developed are felt to measure different aspects of the same general problem (Feldman, 1971; Pervin, 1968).

Of these college assessment methods, those of Pace, Stern, and Pervin were specifically developed to take into account the interactional nature of the relationship of individual personality traits and environmental conditions. The College and University Environment Scale (CUES) and College Characteristics Index (CCI) instruments, developed by Pace and Stern respectively, attempt to describe the climate of a college in terms of "the aggregated perceptions of individuals in the college of the events, conditions, practices, opportunities and pressures of the total environment [Feldman, 1971, p. 52]." The Transactional Analysis of Personality-Environment (TAPE) instrument of Pervin attempts to measure the college environment by focusing on the way students as individuals and as groups perceive the environment. It is Pervin's contention that typical analyses using instruments such as the College Characteristics Index or the College and University Environment Scale fail to place sufficient attention on the interactions or transactions among parts of the university system (students, faculty, and administration).

The use of the College and University Environment Scale by Chickering *et al.* (1969) has permitted comparisons across colleges, while Stern (1965) has used the College Characteristics Index to perform comparisons of colleges and comparisons of student characteristics across different colleges. While the CCI and the CUES provide considerable information on the college "climate," the use of essentially normative results tends to merge the data so as to make analyses of student subgroups and differing college subenvironments difficult. Given the importance of the interactional nature of the relation of individual characteristics to different elements of the environment, the normative presentations in the CCI and the CUES appear to be a serious problem.

The TAPE procedure developed by Pervin (1967a, 1967b) is based on the use of an expanded semantic differential method that provides for the rating of self, students, college, and ideal college on the same scales. Using this procedure Pervin has been able to demonstrate that students who reported a discrepancy between ratings of self and college, and self and other students, had a higher probability of dropping out for nonacademic reasons, felt themselves to be more out of place, and were more dissatisfied with nonacademic aspects of life at their college (Pervin, 1968). The TAPE procedure, by its very design, makes analysis of transactions between parts of the campus more readily performed. The use of the discrepancy scores also permits studies of different campus subgroups in terms of similar perceptions of self or college, faculty, and administration. By defining subgroups in this way, by similar perceptions, subsequent campus environmental analyses may be more sensitive than defining subgroups on some *a priori* bases, e.g., freshman, College Board scores, etc., where variance in self and college perceptions remains unaccounted for. Clearly, future research efforts in this area may demonstrate the merit of this basis for subgroup classifications.

The "interaction" model of student and college fit has been discussed and several methods of assessing college environments have been reviewed which have been derived from this model. Stress, it has been suggested, grows out of those situations where the individual's needs and goals are incongruent with the characteristics and demands of the college environment or subenvironment in which the student finds himself. Some support for the interaction model and for stress associated with a poor student-environment fit has been noted in the dropout literature. The model also provides a useful perspective in understanding research findings related to curriculum and to faculty characteristics (Pervin, 1968). Given the usefulness of this conceptual model in understanding important processes within higher education, one may quite reasonably wonder whether this model and the specific instruments derived from it may lead to methods for identifying and reducing stresses in the college environment.

One attempt to extend the model both conceptually and methodologically into the areas of campus ecology and environmental design comes from recent work by Kaiser (1971a). Kaiser has developed what he calls a design philosophy for campus environments. In it he develops seven main points. These are: 1) A transactional relationship exists between college students and their campus environment, i.e., the students shape the environment and are shaped by it; 2) for the purposes of environmental design, the shaping properties of the campus environment are primary; students, however, are still viewed as active, choice-making agents who may resist, transform, or nullify environmental influences; 3) the campus environment consists of all the stimuli that impinge upon the student's sensory modalities and includes physical, chemical, biological, and social stimulation; 4) every student possesses a wide spectrum of possible behaviors. A campus environment may be designed to facilitate or inhibit any one of these behaviors. The campus may be intentionally designed to provide *opportunities, incentives,* and *reinforcements* for growth and development; 5) students will attempt to cope with any educational environment in which they are placed. If the environment is not compatible with the students, the students may react negatively or fail to develop desirable qualities; 6) because of the wide range of individual differences among students, fitting the campus environment to the students requires the creation of a variety of campus subenvironments. There is an attempt to design not only for the normative students but also for the deviant students; 7) every campus has a design, even if the administration, faculty, and students have not planned it or are not consciously aware of it (Kaiser, 1971a, pp. 5–6). These points summarize a number of issues presented earlier in the discussion of the student-environment fit concepts. Importantly, however, Kaiser extends the interactional concepts into a number of policy statements. First, one must accept the fact that the campus environment has an impact on all those who are encompassed by it. Second, attempts must be made to understand the nature of the possibly "implicit" campus design and to understand the diversity of students' needs, values, and behaviors. Third, attempts must be made to design for students rather than assuming that normative or random planning is satisfactory for all. Lastly, diversity in planning is necessary in fitting the environment to the student. But planned diversity in campus subenvironments is not a product of guessing or making *a priori* assumptions. It is based on careful attempts to study the transactions of students with the environment with the aim of isolating specific environmental elements that are stressful or counterproductive to student development.

One such attempt is being developed by Kaiser (1971b) as a procedure for "mapping" the campus environment. Basically, Kaiser's procedure is an extension of that developed by Pervin. Kaiser asks students to complete the

TAPE ratings for self and college. After the rating of each concept on the college scales, students are asked to supply a "structural referent" from the college environment which corresponds to the rating just made. For instance, if the concept friendly-unfriendly was rated, the student would then indicate what element in the environment corresponded to the rating on the semantic differential scale. By collecting a broad sample of student responses, Kaiser hopes to develop a "consensually validated environment [1971a]." Thus, not only does this procedure yield a distribution of perceptions of self and the environment, but the environmental ratings will be linked to some set of structural elements. The intention here is not to determine some normative responses, but rather to look for clusterings of perceptions and environmental elements that will yield classes of idiosyncratic student perceptions, and groupings of those environmental elements associated with the various semantic-differential concepts. This mapping technique may then articulate students' subgroups based both on perceptions, and different structural referent groupings which may indicate subenvironments. Such information would be highly useful in any attempts at intentional or deliberate planning. Minimally, such efforts could be made to identify and change those aspects of the environment students find noxious.

In addition to the enormous amount of information this engineering approach assumes, it is not without its value judgments and ethical problems. Kaiser suggests students either be given a choice of environments or that the students be assigned to an environment. With the choice of environment strategy, there is the question as to whether students are aware of their weaknesses and strengths so as to make accurate judgments and choices. Next there is the problem of the student who makes a poor choice. Will he have the awareness that it was the choice of the specific environment that is the problem, and will he be able to isolate the difficulty and move to the appropriate setting? With the assignment method there is the question of whether any other person or group of instruments can determine, better than the student himself, the appropriate environmental choice. With both of these methods there is the issue of whether campus environments can be designed with sufficient flexibility to permit awareness of other environments and to foster movement among them. Lastly, one must consider the problem of stress itself. Should the aim of planning be to reduce all stresses or is some level of stress optimal or useful for learning to deal with future stress? One possible criticism of the social engineering model could be that it fosters flight away from distressful situations rather than fostering encounters to reduce the stress. How accurately will this reflect the nature of options and opportunities outside a planned university system? It appears then that some of the most difficult issues in the social engineering process will be the establishment of priorities and values within the designed environment. It may be argued, however, that a careful continuing discussion of campus priorities may in itself be a healthy process for higher education.

Conclusions

The conceptual model developed in this paper has centered around the view that students have a transactional relationship with the college environment. The model has been shown to be useful in understanding some important areas within higher education including student stress and student development. The model, stated in one way or another, appears in so many diverse research efforts that one may view it as a general research perspective. In the college environment context, the concept suggests research that focuses on the complex interrelationships between student characteristics and environmental features. Such research may increase the present understanding of the processes and outcomes of higher education from the student development standpoint.

While the interactional models have great intuitive appeal, the research efforts based on the model are not without difficult methodological and conceptual problems. Pervin (1968) has outlined a number of these issues. What is worthy of some further discussion is the issue of whether one should consider the perceived or "actual" environment. Pervin's TAPE instrument considers only the perceived environment. While this is consistent with the theoretical positions Pervin follows, there remains the question of whether such data will be most useful in understanding the processes within the university system. One possible alternative to the perceptually-based research methods may be efforts that extend research on the reciprocal influence process discussed by Bandura (1969) into the area of student-environmental interactions. Clearly much of the above discussion makes relevant those research efforts that attempt to demonstrate how the behavior of students comes to influence the environment and, reciprocally, how the controlling aspects of the college environment come to alter the students' behavior. As Bandura (1969) states, "individuals far from being ruled by an imposing environment, play an active role in constructing their own reinforcement contingencies through their characteristic modes of response [p. 46]." It therefore appears crucial that any discussion of student-environmental fit must discuss how different individuals and different college subenvironments interact to produce various outcomes in rewards, opportunities, and options. Behaviorally-oriented research may provide a useful contrast to the perceptual methods cited above. While Pervin (1968) suggests the use of both methods until one or the other proves most useful for specific situations, a more desirable strategy might be to initiate studies that attempt to relate perceptual and behavior findings in some systematic way.

Given that the transactional model has been found to be useful in understanding diverse areas of the student-environmental relationship, it is difficult to envision educational policy being determined without consideration of the relevance of these models. Yet many of the policies that determine much of the college environment are developed in isolation from these concepts (Falk, 1971). There is general agreement that different kinds of students respond more favorably to various kinds of class atmospheres or instructional settings, yet little effort is made on most campuses to vary elements of the instructional and evaluation processes systematically. The lack of sensitivity to these issues in educational planning and in recently developed management systems in higher education frustrates student growth and development and limits the success of the university in transmitting knowledge, fostering creativity, and developing human potential. Uniformity of methods and environments is not an appropriate response to diversity on the campus. Increased accessibility to higher education, as some have urged, will mean increased diversity. It is no longer sufficient simply to accept student diversity; the college and university environment must be planned to respond effectively to it, both in its formal program and in its supportive services. Those who work in the student services and student research areas as well as students themselves must begin to collaborate with those who set and review policies and priorities. Where the linkages are absent for such collaboration efforts should be made to establish them. A model for such collaboration has been outlined by Bloom (1971a, 1971b). The quality and responsiveness of the educational environment is a just concern for all members of the college or university community. For as the interactional model suggests, environmental features will in part determine individual outcomes.

In studying the college dropout, Hirsch and Keniston (1970) have noted that "dropping out of college may be, in part, one way in which students with 'atypical' developmental schedules and problems can cope with the pressures of a college geared to the 'typical' student. The high proportion of college students who discontinue or interrupt their education may in part reflect the fact that most students are, in terms of their colleges, 'atypical' [p. 19]."

REFERENCES

Astin, A. W. *The college environment.* Washington, D. C.: American Council on Education, 1968.

Bandura, A. *Principles of behavior modification.* New York: Holt, Rinehart & Winston, 1969.

Bloom, B. L. Proposal for the Center for the Study of the University Community. Office of Student Relations, University of Colorado, 1971a, mimeographed.

Bloom, B. L. Problems of ecology on the college campus: The socio-cultural environment. *Journal of the American College Health Association,* 1971b, *20,* 128–131.

Chickering, A. W., McDowell, J., & Campagna, D. Institutional differences and student development. *Journal of Educational Psychology,* 1969, *60,* 315–326

Falk, D. I. Social change and student development. Paper presented at the Western Interstate Commission for Higher Education meetings on Mental Health Services and the Changing University Community, Claremont, California, December, 1971.

Feldman, K. A. Measuring college environments: Some uses of path analysis. *American Educational Research Journal,* 1971, *8,* 51–70.

Hirsch, S., & Keniston, K. Psychosocial issues in talented college dropouts. *Psychiatry,* 1970, *33,* 1–20.

Kaiser, L. Campus ecology: Implications for environmental design. Paper presented at the Western Interstate Commission for Higher Education meetings on Campus Ecology and Mental Health Epidemiology, Santa Fe, New Mexico, 1971a.

Kaiser, L. Personal communication, 1971b.

Kelly, J. G. Toward an ecological conception of preventive interventions. In D. Adelson & B. Kalis (Eds.),

Community psychology and mental health: Perspectives and challenges. Scranton, Pa.: Chandler Publishing Co., 1970.

Leininger, M. Interfaces of the university cultures and society with focus upon cultural values and conflict areas. Paper presented at the Western Interstate Commission for Higher Education meetings on Mental Health Services and the Changing University Community, Lake Tahoe, California, September, 1971.

Lewin, K. *Field theory in social science.* New York: Harper & Row, 1951.

Murray, H. A. *Explorations in personality.* New York: Oxford University Press, 1938.

Pace, C. R. *Preliminary technical manual: College and University Environment Scales.* Princeton, N.J.: Educational Testing Services, 1963.

Pace, C. R. *College and University Environment Scales (second edition), Technical manual.* Princeton, N.J.: Educational Testing Services, 1969.

Pace, C. R., & Stern, G. An approach to the measurement of psychological characteristics of college environments. *Journal of Educational Psychology,* 1958, *49,* 269–277.

Pervin, L. A. Identification, identity, and the college dropout. *Journal of the American College Health Association,* 1966, *14,* 158–164.

Pervin, L. A. A twenty-college study of student X college interaction using TAPE (transactional analysis of personality and environment); Rationale, reliability, and validity. *Journal of Educational Psychology,* 1967a, *58,* 290–302.

Pervin, L. A. Satisfaction and perceived self-environment similarity: A semantic differential study of student-college interaction. *Journal of Personality,* 1967b, *35,* 623–634

Pervin, L. A. Performance and satisfaction as a function of individual-environment fit. *Psychological Bulletin,* 1968, *69,* 56–68.

Pervin, L. A., & Rubin, D. Student dissatisfaction with college and the college dropout: A transactional approach. *Journal of Social Psychology,* 1967, *72,* 285–295.

Shaw, K. A. Accuracy of expectation of a university's environment as it relates to achievement, attrition, and change of degree objective. *Journal of College Student Personnel,* 1968, *9,* 44–48.

Snyder, B. R. Student stress. In T. F. Lunsford (Ed.), *Campus cultures.* Boulder: Western Interstate Commission for Higher Education, 1963. Pp. 27–38.

Stern, G. Environments for learning. In N. Sanford (Ed.), *The American college: A psychological and social interpretation of the higher learning.* New York: Wiley, 1962a.

Stern, G. The measurement of psychological characteristics of students and learning environments. In S. Messick & J. Ross (Eds.), *Measurement in personality and cognition.* New York: Wiley, 1962b.

Stern, G. Student ecology and the college environment. *Journal of Medical Education,* 1965, *40,* 132–154.

2. Psychodynamics of Development During the College Years

JOSEPH KATZ

At about the time of entering college most people embark upon the second phase of adolescence. The second phase, though it is less immediately obvious, is as dramatic as the first. The first phase (Blos, 1962) was dominated by the sudden spurt of bodily growth, the powerful reawakening and intensification of the sexual drive and its physical accompaniments, the onset of the menses and seminal emission. It brings a powerful intensification of emotions of all kinds, embarrassment, anger, rebelliousness. The world is seen in stark colors of good and evil. There is a strong tendency to differentiate oneself from other people, peers as well as those who are younger and older. Regressive tendencies make childhood inviting, while the growing ego orients itself towards independence and fights the seduction of being taken care of.

This chapter relies heavily on the author's research studies of personality development during the college years, particularly on the longitudinal study of Berkeley and Stanford students which followed the 1961 entrants through their four college years by means of interviews, personality inventories, questionnaires, and other instruments. The Berkeley-Stanford study is reported in Joseph Katz and associates, *No Time for Youth*, San Francisco: Jossey-Bass, 1968. The findings of that study are consonant with those of other investigators (see the literature cited in the references).

43

Adults, when viewed with the passions of the adolescent, seem feeble in their emotionality. When judged by the ego reaching for greater autonomy, they seem compromising, conformist. On the cognitive side they seem not precise and knowledgeable enough to young minds that are beginning to grasp their environment with verve and the powers of first impressions. Some people even during the first phase of adolescence go through deeply involving experiments with sex, or drugs, daring or bizarre actions of one sort or another—to the great astonishment of their parents who find it difficult to recongnize in the new behavior the charming child of a year or two ago. For most adolescents the intensity stays on the level of fantasy, strong feeling, and recurring verbal hassles with parents and siblings. When maturation is achieved towards the end of the first phase of adolescence, the enlarged body, though not entirely brought under control, becomes an accustomed fact, and so does sexual striving, though it remains for many a mystery, a source of tension, and a half-acknowledged anticipation of pleasure.

In the second phase of adolescence relations with peers, parents, and other adults remain a source of conflict and a task for development—at high levels of intensity. While one's own body is now a more familiar object, the external world becomes more of a problem; for what the adolescent now faces are his oncoming tasks as a member of the world of work, separation from home, and the establishment of his own sexual identity, including the anticipation of marriage and other sexual and interpersonal roles. The battle again is within himself and with the external world. In regard to himself he faces the uncertainties of whether and how he will make it in the adult world, anxieties intensified in our society because the adolescent, particularly if he goes to college, is given so little opportunity for participating in the world of work (Katz, 1968, Ch. 1).

When the adolescent looks at the world he faces a situation he has not made, beset with strife and destructiveness. He sees reflected in the world the emotions he has had so much difficulty taming in his infancy and now again in the intensifications of adolescence. The world seems to fit poorly with his idealism which is as yet little spoiled by the struggle for economic security and status. The world also seems discrepant with the personal dignity, freedom, and caring he may have experienced in his own family. Since the 1960's the struggles and anxieties of adolescents in college have been further intensified by the fact that many students no longer view their colleges as aids for their own development, but rather as representatives of a system in which authorities, faculty included, do not respond to the needs of people under their care but prefer to satisfy the interest of their own particular guilds and private domains.

The inner and outer uncertainties of the second phase of adolescence make it a time when the personality is particularly indeterminate and fluid. It is a time when past commitments have been loosened and new commitments have not yet been made. This, coupled with the strong drive for independence, makes it the most opportune time in the human life cycle for a self-engendered remaking of the personality. The first shaping of personality in infancy was involuntary, determined by the values, attitudes, and psychological make-up of parents and other available figures in the childhood environment. At adolescence the individual has the opportunity to remake himself in accordance with dispositions that may have been neglected or thwarted in his family environment and in accordance with the needs of the world he is about to enter, a world often different from the one his parents confronted when they were at his stage in life.

SEPARATION FROM HOME

As the adolescent prepares to enter the world, his parents may not easily be suitable as models for him. If they have been too inhibitory, his growing autonomy will seek for some release from external as well as internalized bonds. But even if they have been more nurturant, he still looks for possibilities beyond those of the emotional range and life style of his family. Hence the need to leave home, to find other models, and to seek out fresh experience. There is some implicit wisdom in our educational institutions. Just as school begins at five or six, when children enter the phase of "latency," the period when there is a diminution of the intense sexual and aggressive emotionality of childhood in favor of more reality-oriented industry, so separation from home is much facilitated by the residential college. Others do not sever childhood bonds until later. Some never do.

The separation from home is, like much adolescent behavior, two-headed. It is progressive, oriented towards the assumption of mature independence; it is beset at the same time by anxieties engendered by the giving up of the comforts of earlier security and dependence. Particularly in our society when parental ideology stresses their children's independence and freedom of choosing—there are less direct parental messages that embody much more definite expectations—freshmen will often hide from themselves and others their separation anxiety. Observations of freshmen reveal many symptoms of separation anxiety, among them a worried concern about not being at home just when one or the other parent needs them—a projection often of their own need onto their parents—or disappointments when on their first trip home during the freshman year they find their former room taken over by another sibling, their belongings moved to an attic.

The first year also witnesses a good deal of transfer of attachment from the home to the college. Many students come to describe college as their new home, the home of the mass barracks that characterize both higher education institutions and the army in America, a home that three years later they may have difficulty leaving; a few usually hang on for additional years in the old environment of alma mater. During the first year away from home, students learn to take care of their own needs in more independent ways, regulating their hours, determining their budget, making new friends, finding new adult models. Much is ambiguous and the laundry that may be sent back home is an indication of the continuing dependence.

All these developments lay the basis for a confrontation which frequently takes place in the summer after the freshman year when students return home for a more extended period of time. By this point they have implicitly acquired a certain amount of self-determination. They feel, however, that their parents react to them still in the old ways, e.g., trying to regulate the times when they are supposed to be home, how they are to dress, to keep their room, what ideas they may appropriately express. This gives rise to mutual harrassment. The children usually "win" this battle and the reports from the second college summer are different and give an indication of learning on both sides. Parents are beginning to accept their children's separation and independent adulthood and their children are learning to be less provocative and more tolerant of their parents' differences from themselves which they begin to see as conditioned by the different experiences and life styles of their parents.

This process is a gradual one and extends over all of the four college years. When one compares the statements of freshmen about their parents with those of seniors, one is frequently struck by how very differently the same people are described. In the interest of his growing differentiation and independence the adolescent has greatly exaggerated those characteristics in his parents from which he is struggling away or which are feared tendencies and temptations in himself. There is a "flexing of the muscle" as the adolescent discovers in himself powers of reasoning or of social consciousness superior to those he perceives in his own parents. There is a settling of old scores, residues of antagonisms originating in imaginary or real thwartings of his desires when he was younger.

As he becomes surer of his identity, the adolescent can take a different look at his parents and, when things are favorable, reestablish a relationship with them on the basis of a new equality and a respect founded in his parents' real accomplishments and not in the omnipotent expectations of childhood. For instance, a woman student interviewed by the author in her freshman year described her mother as unintellectual and quite unaffectionate. The same student reported herself in her senior year as exchanging books and ideas with her mother, and she became somewhat rhapsodical about the loving relationship between her parents, giving some vivid descriptions of their caressing each other in front of the fireplace. In the years between there had been many storms when this young woman had tried to chart her own occupational course and define her ideology in the face of opposition from her parents. Mark Twain expressed it all very well when he had one of his adolescents say he was much surprised how much the old man had learned in four years.

CONDITIONS OF CHANGE

What we have said thus far describes the adolescent's past, his desire for change or sometimes even transformation. The adolescent often enters college with considerable enthusiasm and readiness for change. But the degree of activeness with which freshmen expect to work towards these changes differs considerably. For some, the expectation is relatively passive, the desire to be stimulated or even waiting to be discovered. The student's past schooling may not have strongly cultivated his tendency towards activity. A combination of boredom, living up to peer expectations, and the injunction to be a good boy or girl in order to make it into the college of one's choice may have furthered a tendency to be relatively passive. But there are experiences waiting for the freshman that may jolt him out of previous adaptations. There is the impact of peers from different social or geographical origins, or peers with different ideologies or different personality dispositions. There are the professors who represent a wider spectrum of ideologies and attitudes than he may have encountered either at home or in high school. There are the new living arrangements in the dormitory with masses of people around, with noise, with late hours, with the direct confrontations of raucous, aggressive, or even bizarre behavior quite different from the individual room he may have had in his parental home. There is the wider range of ideas and of esthetic experiences that the extra-curricular life may bring him to. There are enlarged opportunities for travel, field work, and exposure to life in settings different from those of the suburban or urban home.

In a general way one can say that what develops or changes a student the most is his having experiences in activities and roles quite different from those before he entered college. Thus a student who works as a professional apprentice, or engages in a research project, or becomes a political leader, or renders social service, or goes on a political mission experiences himself as an agent and may develop capacities which before he may have barely suspected. A lesser degree of impact is due not to direct experience but to confrontation with the different experiences of others. Thus, closeness to a professor can lead to imitation, identification, and an eventual adoption of some selected traits that modify the personality. Study abroad and exposure to different people and different ways of behaving or, at home, the exposure to students with different religious and political views or differing attitudes to other people, e.g., greater amounts of trust or intelligent mistrust, all lead to modifications of the personality; but they do so more indirectly because in themselves they have only stimulus value.

Opportunities for transforming experiences vary with the college and the particular subgroup to which a student belongs; they also vary with the individual student's capacity for autonomy. Some of the changes can be only imitative and remain superficial, a function of the student's conformity with the college environment. For instance, some of the ideological "liberalism" displayed by undergraduates is a function of the environment (Korn, 1968, pp. 179 ff.; Newcomb, *et al.*, 1967) and may be dissipated once students enter other environments that are not supportive of these same values.

THE INFLUENCE OF PEERS

A very potent factor in the student's transformation is his relationships with his peers (Feldman and Newcomb, 1969, pp. 236–248). Given the nature of the college environment, with its limited access to adults, there is an almost natural generational distance built in, encouraging a stronger reliance of peers upon each other. The influence of peers cannot, however, be ascribed to circumstances alone. It is also founded in the adolescent's need to differentiate himself from the adult world by some alliance, at times rebellious, with people in his own generation who have shared his experiences and who are like him in their aspirations.

Emotionally and cognitively, the impact of peers is of great educational influence upon student development. Beginning in the bull sessions of the freshman year and continuing in other associations, including shared work in study projects in the laboratory or the field, peers are the educators of each other. In this education the often exclusive emphasis of the classroom on cognitive factors is bypassed and peer education is both intellectual and affective. It includes responding to the character of the people one interacts with, a sense of the person who is behind the statements, the meaning of the statements in that person's life, a sense of his life style, his family origins, his cynicisms and idealisms. Atheistic and religious fresh-

men confronting each other in a bull session will not necessarily adopt each other's position, but they will each
come out with a refined view of their values stances. Occupational choices may be determined in observations of
peers, exposure to their homes, and discussions which
scrutinize motivations and aspirations (White, 1966, pp.
48ff.). Groups of students meeting in a dormitory room
discussing politics or poetry may be hammering out a
different attitude to life. They may share thoughts on
experiences or things they have seen or read, in part to
show off before each other and in part to underpin attitudes with a base in the objective facts of reality.

The impression should not be given that conditions on
the college scene are even nearly optimal for the full
utilization of peer influence. There is much isolation of
students from each other, loneliness, and superficiality in
relationships. Part of this is self-protective because development takes time and calls into play many defenses.
Many a student assigned at random to others as a freshman will flee them as soon as he can, simply because their
values and personalities were too far removed from his
own present possibilities. One of the great appeals of the
activism of the 1960's was the opportunities it provided
for community. In the demonstrations and the sit-ins, students were sharing a common objective, were interacting
intensely, and had the chance for much greater knowledge of each other than is possible in the classroom or
even the dormitory. Moreover, the planning and coordination for a common social purpose provided a sense of
social nexus that is rare in the individualistic upbringing
and manners of our society.

There is a further obstacle to the realization of the student's aspirations for greater relatedness to others. This
lies in the student's way of handling aggression, including
hostile aggression. In his relationship with others, the student experiences many feelings of invidious comparison,
of competitiveness, of jolts or shocks to his value system,
the fear of insignificance from seeming one small individ-

ual in the mass society of the dormitory and campus. Because the rules governing relations are often less well defined than they were in the parental home, the student may find himself at a loss regarding what to do with a roommate whose patterns of behavior interfere with his own study and leisure activities. He may be at a loss about what to do with a visiting student who comes to his room at an inopportune time. He may choose to spend much of his time outside of his own room rather than telling a roommate about behavior that is disturbing or offensive to him (Katz, 1968, pp. 44–45).

Students confuse assertiveness with hostility—a confusion perhaps particularly characteristic of American culture. This confusion is in part due to the fact that felt hostilities are not easily allowed access to consciousness and, even less, appropriate expression to the object of hostility. Submergence of feelings about other people is partially responsible for the distance and lack of involvement that students have with each other. The great attraction of encounter groups for students in recent years lies strongly in the promise they hold out of greater openness of feelings towards each other; however, the sledgehammer tactics often used in encounter groups prevent a realization of these hopes for many.

Sexual Development

Preeminent in the area of peer relationships is the establishment of sexual identity. Our society, when it maps out its official goals for education in all stages of life, constantly underplays the centrality of this task; at the same time the repressed returns in the constant preoccupations with sex in advertising, comics, jokes, popular arts. The adolescent emanates from a society and a family in which sex may not have been talked about directly, been kept under some cover while the popular media have painted it in lurid and seductive colors. This situation makes it

harder for him to integrate sex into the rest of his personality, to develop mature sexuality, namely, the establishment of a relationship with a member of the opposite sex
which involves a sense of who oneself is, understanding of
a person different from oneself, mutuality in which there
is respect for differences, and a capacity for mutual empathy and joint action (Group for the Advancement of Psychiatry, 1965).

The achievement of a relatively secure and circumscribed identity is a precondition for mutuality and intimacy. The adolescent proceeds by stages, and he tends
first to develop his standing among peers of the same sex
before he ventures out more fully into the area of relations with the opposite sex. Until recently, it was quite
common for many freshman men to keep much distance
from the opposite sex. For freshmen women it was common to date frequently and with many different men. The
women needed to convince themselves of their attrac-
tiveness and desirability; at the same time they would not
let the men get very close because they perceived this as
a threat to their being able to accomplish the tasks of
intellectual, academic, or vocational development they
had set for themselves in their college years. Only gradually and towards the junior year did students move towards more stable relationships and towards the
establishment of sexual intimacy. Less than half of the
women and about half of the men on campuses studied by
the author had established sexual intimacy even by the
end of the senior year.

This has changed now. Intercourse is more frequent
earlier. This means that students are exposed earlier to
the depth and often the agonies of the attempts at closeness. They are exposed earlier to the guilt that sexual
relations may arouse, to the close ties that the sexual impulse often has to aggressive, if not sado-masochistic, tendencies (Katz, 1972). This earlier exposure accentuates
the preeminent fact about sex, that it is not primarily a
physical release but involves the charting of relationships

between people that involve all dimensions of the person, from his infantile tendencies, fantasies, and longings to his need for sharing his thoughts, displaying his abilities, developing his responsiveness, getting encouragement for his aspirations and idealisms, making a mark in the world, being deeply appreciated by somebody close to him who cannot be deceived by mask, sweet talk, bravado, and yet will give love to what is really there.

This is a gigantic task and the current generation is paying a price in anxiety for having to confront some of these problems without the benefit of a more prolonged moratorium by which relationships can be dealt with more playfully, as they were in the more or less ritualized "date" of the past. At the same time there is now more opportunity for educational institutions to exercise their developmental function while the students are within their domain. The possibility exists that young people will deepen their capacity for relationships before commitments are made and hence commitments might be made to more appropriate partners and with deeper experience in relationships.

Perhaps the overriding fact about current developments is the much greater autonomy of women. Women in our society, and perhaps generally, have tended to be more psychologically-minded, more sensitive to feelings, more in touch with what is below consciousness. Now that marriage is becoming less a sign of status and the birth rate and desire for larger families have shrunk, college women have been stressing very much more the need for relationship. They now engage in sexual activities earlier and more frequently, and they quite freely testify to the pleasure they take in sex and the conjoint emotional closeness. They thus are putting the pressure on the men for a greater scrutiny of the quality of the men's emotional involvement. They reject being treated as sex objects. This challenges the men to let the women become their teachers in those areas where their own sensitivities have been underdeveloped. The signs are that college men are responding in larger numbers to this challenge.

ADULT MODELS

We have already indicated that one of the major tasks facing the college student is the establishment of a new identity in distinction from the one given in his original family situation. This does not exclude continuation in more or less conscious ways of parental influence. It affects, for instance, the occupational choice process in which students often conform to the ambitions and expectations of their parents (Katz, *et al.*, 1969). Parental influence will emerge even more strongly later when the children themselves become marital partners and parents and tend to fall back on identities learned over the many years at home. Nevertheless, because the college years are a time for remaking of the person, adult models are sought out for fresh identifications beyond those provided in the original family.

One form of using the adult as a model is the attempt at an imitative adoption of many of his traits. For instance, a student may try to imitate the styles of thinking, the leisure time activities, the predilections, sometimes even the manner of dress or ways of walking of a favorite adult that he has come in close contact with. These imitations usually are short-lived. Freshmen in particular will flock to people with strong dissentious or radical views because they are at such variance with the more placid views of their earlier environment. These models are transitional objects of identification. The tendency over the college years is not for wholesale identification, but rather for a more selective use of certain parts of adult behavior as stimuli to one's own growth and identity. Students get affected differently. One student can appreciate and learn from the precise theoretical articulations of a professor, while another will also adopt something of the hostile or even sadistic manner of interrogation that this professor displays in the classroom.

For the purposes of development there is the need for more than sheer presence of a model displaying himself to the student. There is the need for the model to be responsive to the student as an individual, his particular strivings, competencies, and shortcomings. There is need for encouragement, approval, and evaluation of his work. Learning and development take place at a deeper level wherever such responsiveness exists, as in the apprentice-master relationship of a student and professor working together on a research project, particularly if this relationship is further deepened by the student's access to the professor personally, including his home surroundings. There is a dearth of such opportunity in the colleges. Professors are often just remote figures on the lecture platform, so that even the simplest modeling is difficult.

There is a further problem from the point of view of developmental needs. Professors are only one segment of humanity, often a very intellectualized segment. Students, on the other hand, span the whole spectrum of intellectual, practical, esthetic, political, and social inclinations. To develop in their own terms they need access to a broad spectrum of adults who can serve as models to encourage the development of their individual potential. Lawyers, businessmen, administrators, and many others are usually not very prominent in the society of the college. This lack of models is particularly flagrant for women students who are excluded from direct acquaintance with the work life of professional women or, for that matter, of women who at home exemplify successful accomplishments in the domestic sphere.

When we speak of adult models, it is important to keep the adolescent's ambivalence to authority in mind. Students on many campuses have demanded greater access to faculty. On inspection, this demand often turns out to be two-sided. What is wanted is both approval, encouragement, and more relevant instruction from elders and at the same time distance from faculty out of a desire not to be under their control and criticism. The ambivalence is rooted in the simultaneous striving for dependence and independence. Demands for access to faculty also can have a provocative connotation because the adolescent

senses the faculty's guilty conscience over their insuffi-
cient attention to their students. Administrative and faculty awareness of student ambivalences could avoid the
twin dangers of pseudo-closeness and of hostile or repressive confrontation.

THE PASSAGE THROUGH COLLEGE

Students during the college years move from more absolutistic and less qualified perceptions and attitudes to
those that are more differentiated, more complex, more
tolerant, more flexible (Perry, 1970). This holds for cognitive, emotional, aesthetic, and ethical development. The
freshman is more inhibited in his impulse expression, and
his conscience still is more rigid and punitive than that of
the upperclassman. He is passionate but his passion still is
much under the domination of the superego. Hence he
can be harshly condemnatory of adults whom he sees as
compromised if not outrightly corrupted, and he may
view social conditions as the product of evil malice, ne-
glecting the complex impersonal forces of institutions that
prove themselves difficult to modify by will alone.

The freshman resembles the authoritarian, making
sharp distinctions between ingroup and outgroup, having
a harsh, if not punitive, orientation towards those who
belong to the social or ideological outgroup, casting his
beliefs in a dogmatic form, and decrying as "phony" those
who deviate from his puristic conception of the world
(Sanford, 1962). Cognitively too, his thinking has an absolutistic cast, looking for truth and certainty and not yet
quite aware of the tentative and hypothetical nature of
even our more warranted scientific conclusions, not to
speak of many of the ideas we hold in the "softer" fields
of knowledge.

The freshman only appears certain. His absolutism and
his dogmatism are a function of his insecurity, his desire
for an assurance that he does not yet possess. This insecu-

rity expresses itself in his relations with other people, particularly his peers among whom he seeks acceptance and self-validation. Moreover, his powers of interaction with others, of empathy and understanding for psychological differences, are as yet underdeveloped. His relations with others may still have the cast of self-display rather than of interaction. One can observe conversations among freshmen in which there is less meshing of what is said than biding of time until each can appear on the stage having his say.

Freshman talk is often an expression of developmental tasks and anxieties. Sex, religion, the family, authority are some of its main staples. These topics are not abstractions for the freshman but topics in which his thinking reverberates his strong emotions, anxieties, and premature attempts at closure that give what he says an absolutistic cast. He often cannot look at these problems with the detachment required for more objective sorting of evidence, for more careful attempts at scientific or theoretical formulation. One might say that the freshman still is in an ideological stage of development and that he has not yet arrived at the theoretical stage. Teachers often fail to recognize the fact of this ideological stage and hence, by premature discouragement of the freshman's own gropings towards articulation and by setting up standards that appear too cold and too difficult, make him doubt his thinking capacities rather than enticing him to develop them. This failure of response goes hand in hand with the frequent disregard of the freshman's desperate need for self-esteem. A teacher's disapproving or downgrading stance in the name of "standards" which may be more appropriate for a later stage or perhaps appropriate only to the community of the teacher's own peers has a demoralizing effect upon freshmen.

One by one the student over the college years attempts to meet the challenges put before him. He discovers competencies that he did not expect, develops those that he brought with him. He develops a more realistic conception of what he can do, giving up some of the expectations that in the overblown idealism and perhaps self-punitiveness of his earlier years led to the setting of too harsh, too comprehensive tasks for himself. He needs less to conform to the expectations of others. He finds he can master academic subject matter. He often finds that academic tasks are easier than he anticipated after he has acquired certain habits of reading, culling information, and making generalizations, particularly those that are important to his professor.

After trial and error, and often pain, he learns to find members of his own sex and the opposite sex with whom he can have a comfortable relationship. The diminution of interpersonal anxiety means that he can pay more attention to other people's feelings and make a closer scrutiny of his own behavior, all these establishing "virtuous circles" easing his relationship with others. His moral, social, and religious views in the upperclass years have more definiteness and firmness, but they are no longer harsh and he has more tolerance for people who take different positions.

OCCUPATIONAL DEVELOPMENT

Particularly for the men, and increasingly for the women, occupational status is an important part of student identity strivings. Children from a very early age are asked what they will become when they are grown up. They are forced to give answers before they have the prerequisite experience or an adequate sense of their own capacities to give an intelligent answer. The consequence may be a rush into a premature choice, particularly when there are strong parental or other social expectations to which the individual is compliant. Adolescents who remain in a state of occupational uncertainty experience a special anxiety because of what they perceive to be the social expectations that they be more certain. The collegiate system adds to, rather than mitigates, this anxiety. Under the collegiate system, four years are spent not so much in exposure to the world of work as in exposure to a variety of subject matters that in themselves can be engrossing but that, except for further academicians, portray little of the substance of other activities in the world of work. Less than one percent of entering freshmen nationwide expect to become college teachers (American Council on Education, 1971). What jobs students hold during the college years, including the summers, afford to only a small minority exposure to occupations they might later wish to enter.

The adolescent also feels anxiety about occupational commitment, as he feels it about other commitments. Occupational commitment carries for him the threat of a limitation of his life space, a diminishing of future possibilities he has entertained in his fantasies, a fear of the "nine-to-five" routine that would no longer make him the adventurer, the explorer, the daydreamer, the pleasure-seeker he has wished to be. He also asks himself anxious questions about whether he has the necessary competence to perform well. If his father or mother or siblings already are high performers, fears about measuring up may be strong. If he is the first in his family to range occupationally beyond his father's position, he will experience the anxiety of outdoing a once feared object. (The difficulty that many people have in finishing their Ph.D. work may have one root in this fear.) In times of job scarcity, there is the more or less realistic concern about being able to win in the competitive race.

The result is that some students cling more or less tenaciously to an occupation they or their parents had chosen for them before they entered college, or cling to it at the expense of being open to the new stimuli and challenges of the college years. Other students experience considerable uncertainty and anxiety. Even at commencement time many will not have made their occupational choice and will look to graduate or professional school or to future work experiences to determine what they might be fitted for. The path towards occupational identity, therefore, shows a considerable amount of drift; vital choices are made without experiential opportunities and psychological awareness of which occupation may be congenial and expressive of one's potential.

Women are particularly handicapped when it comes to making occupational choices. They face restricted opportunities in graduate school and in occupations. They often face an interruption in their occupational development because the years after college are filled with temporary lower-level jobs or the tasks of wifehood and child rearing. This cuts them off from the exploration of their occupational potential and it has saddled many of them with deep uncertainty about their capacities for self-expression and competence in work other than domestic work. Women thus often approach their middle years, after their children have grown, with a lack of self-confidence and sense of autonomy. Even in the child-rearing years, a sense of incompleteness often is more or less directly present. In the last few years, undergraduate women have begun to redefine their ambitions and life plans and society is beginning to respond to their occupational needs more fully.

Societal expectation until now has been that people will settle down in one occupation which becomes their life's work. This has been the expectation even though some individuals have had multiple careers and many more have shifted the nature of their activity within the same career category. At the present time, however, the "one person—one career" pattern is being challenged by the rapid obsolescence of many occupations and the increased speed of redefinitions and shifts within the same occupational category, as when an engineer turns from electronics to salesmanship or administration. The "one man—one career" pattern also can be challenged on psychological grounds because it does not take into account the fact that as people develop, their interests and psycho-

logical dispositions may change so that an occupation chosen at age eighteen or twenty-two may no longer be very
suitable.

Growth of the personality may, for many people, be
dependent on being able to express their indentities
through different forms of work and occupation. Young
people, in their hesitation about occupational commitment, may have been sensing a deficiency in the societal
pattern, fearing an undue narrowing of their chance for
expression and development. Under the favorable economic conditions of the 1960's many young people prolonged their *Wanderjahre*, delayed entry into the job
market, or prolonged their graduate school years for the
sake of increasing the scope of experiences and the activities they would try themselves out on. The aristocratic
principle that youth is not ended until about age thirty
may express a developmental principle which a social
class not under the need of immediately making a living
has been able to put into operation more easily.

REALIGNMENTS IN THE PERSONALITY STRUCTURE

Our account shows that much psychological work is
being done during the college years. One can sum it up
by saying that the senior, in contrast to the freshman, is
a person whose conscience is more humanized, whose
impulse life is more liberated, and whose ego is much
strengthened (Sanford, *et al.*, 1956). The college years
mark a transition from relative dependence towards the
assumption of roles in which people become more fully
contributing members of society, more in charge of regulating their own lives and managing their impulses and
activities. The psychological alignment of the id, ego, and
superego systems in the personality are different at the
end of that period from what they were at its beginning.
The *id system* is changed because there is now a greater
freedom of impulse expression. The sexual impulse is less

hedged by anxiety, restrictions, and over-idealizations and moves towards expression in emotional closeness and physical explorations. There is a similar freeing of aggressive and assertive tendencies.

The capacity of impulse expression is very closely related to developments in the *ego system,* particularly the development of a sense of competence and the ensuing higher self-esteem. Because the ego thinks better of itself, it can now be less fearful or less concerned that hurt might come from other people if certain views and inclinations are being expressed. This growing sense of competence has, first of all, a somatic component. The body has now entered a more stable phase and the young person is habituated to its enlarged size. The sense of comfort is strengthened by physical exercise and by the exhilaration of experiencing one's physical energy, endurance, and vitality. Control of subject matter, whether through the formal curriculum or in intellectual, artistic, or political activities pursued on one's own, further give a sense that one's efforts can lead to accomplishment and mastery. In the social sphere, competence expresses itself in much greater ease of relations with other people, a sense of understanding them better, greater empathy, and the capacity of taking responsibility for others and of caring for them.

There is slow growth away from self-centeredness towards openness for other people's feelings, the growth of the capacity of fostering somebody else's development (Erikson, 1959). A firmer sense of one's own identity, particularly a sense of being a competent self, needs to precede intimacy and caring for others. But when one speaks of intimacy following identity, it is important not to think of these as strictly sequential stages. In many ways the development of both is simultaneous and takes place in all stages of life. But there are shifts in priority. For instance, identity strivings may again take priority when young professionals, faculty included, attempt to establish themselves in their careers.

There are important changes in the *superego system*. The freshman is given to vivid "black and white" divisions of the world. Even a slight compromise with principle may seem phony to him. He expects others and himself to live up to often rigidly conceived concepts of excellence and he is ready for verbal punishment of others or for self-punishment if there is deviation from the standard. His judgment of his own parents tends, as we have seen, to the extreme. Many forces determine his moral absolutism. His ego may not yet be strong enough to control his vigorous impulses with less strict rules. He is defining a more independent personality by trying out new ways of conduct defined in opposition to those that were held by him or by his family earlier. His moral absolutism is far from being only defensive. He is also attempting, with his maturing capacity for conceptualization, to see the world in clearer colors, to see its corruptions and lethargy. Even if overstated, his principles embody fresh ways of meeting the future. Consider the push that young people have recently given to the search for solutions to problems of the environment, of racial justice, of war, and of life style.

Debates with his peers, living with peers of different psychological dispositions and social experiences, confronting in his teachers a wide variety of viewpoints about the same subject matter; these and other experiences help to relativize his own conception of the world and to bring into doubt his former absolutism. All the while his increasing ego strength makes him less resistive to evidence that may undermine an absolutist position, which he may have clung to for the sake of preserving the integrity and boundaries of his own self.

While this relativization is more or less unsettling for many students, it tends to go with a growing recognition that some kind of sorting out among the conflicting claims can be made. First of all, tolerance develops for people who believe or act differently. At first this may go together with the notion that other people's ways might be wrong or, at the very least, not right for one's self. But gradually there seeps in the idea that some of the beliefs or actions of other people might be incorporated into one's own system. Adopting a certain political belief or being friends with a person who was considered socially, emotionally, or ethnically outside of one's class may come to be seen as enriching the ways in which one understands the world, in which one feels and acts. By the senior year, many students' consciences are more reasoned and yet firmer, as distinguished from strident, and conscience reflects the rules that allow people to live together and to be more humane to each other, rather than being a weapon for the aggrandizement of one's self or one's group and the physical or moral humiliation of the outsider.

By contrast with the relative maturity, presence, and poise of the twenty-one-year-old, the seventeen-year-old looks boyish and girlish. The passage of these four years is often marked by crisis. These crises have been called identity crises. But it is important to realize that the identity crisis is not a single dramatic event (though some crises for some people stand out with particular clarity), but rather a succession of little crises. Such crises do reach consciousness in varying degrees. They come in segments. Students do not confront themselves in a wholesale way, but rather tackle this or that aspect of themselves. Academic problems and tasks may loom large at one time, peer relationships or confrontations with authority may loom large at another.

A distinction should be made between normal and extraordinary development during the college years. Under extraordinary development I understand a major shift in the alignment of the psychological systems of the id, ego, and superego. Such extraordinary development would be illustrated by major changes in dependency patterns, impulse control, or access to one's unconscious. They can be induced by the strong impact of peers or adults, by experiences which conflict strongly with previously unchallenged ideas and values, importantly, by a developing capacity for self-scrutiny and honesty with one's self. But such extraordinary developments are rare. In less dramatic forms, development is practically universal during the college years. In addition to the inner forces for growth, development is stimulated by the new role demands made upon people in the passage from seventeen to twenty-one. From relative supervision by parents and their delegates, the student moves into situations in which much of his daily behavior is determined by himself and in which he is expected to contribute rather than to be supervised and sheltered. Nevertheless, fundamental psychological dispositions, though modified, can persist. A person who was dependent on his parents can transfer dependency onto the people in his new environment; a teacher, a boss, a spouse. Dependency can be expressed even in regard to one's own children by making them overly dependent on parental support. Colleges have been very far from utilizing the potential readiness for psychological growth that exists in young people.

Different Patterns of Change

Some people change little during the college years. This seems to result from a combination of environmental factors and the predisposition they bring to college. On the environmental side, the curricular program, the degree of individuality and expressiveness it may or may not favor, and the subgroups to which a student belongs may exert an inhibiting or stimulating influence. Predisposition to a static response seems to be laid early in the development of the person. A child before age five may have come to the conclusion that he is likely to encounter less trouble and maintain the affection or at least benevolence of his parents by doing as he is told and by anticipating their wishes. If such children grow up in an environment that does not do gross violence to their own inclinations and desires, their submissiveness and conformity may not entail too great a cost to their peace of mind. These students are authoritarian in the sense that they depend on more rigid external rules and restrict impulse and imagination. But in contrast to the pure authoritarian, they do not tend to view people different from themselves as bad and as targets of hostile aggression. They constitute something like a psychological middle class who do the work of the college and the society as present structures require it, do it with little complaint, a certain passive enjoyment of conformity, and a decent orientation towards other people. When societies are relatively stable, such people can be highly functional. The question in our times of more rapid social change is whether this disposition is still as functional as it once was.

The pure authoritarian's resistance, if not imperviousness, to change is founded on a more intense and more conflicted impulse life. He tends to be both self-punitive and to project onto the external world some of his own unacceptable impulses which he combats by attacking other people. The pressure of impulse and the anxiety aroused by inner conflict are so strong that the college environment—peers, teachers and ideas—makes little impact and is used to confirm previously held attitudes rather than to modify them. Only a much more deliberate psychological education could ever hope to affect the rigidity of this syndrome. To attempt such modification would seem very desirable because the authoritarians' intensity and sense of mission often disturb their society in disproportion to their numbers.

The authoritarian syndrome seems to have one of its determinants in a parental home in which there were strict demands, but demands in conflict with each other, with father and mother pulling the child in different directions and with disregard to the child's own impulses. By contrast, the more benevolent authoritarian student tends to report his parents as having been in harmony with each other. He has vague or no reports of quarrels or disagreements between mother and father. His descriptions of his parents are in the form of the family romance, father and mother being presented as all-loving, all-good, and knowing best.

Psychological potential for development is a function of the alignment of impulse and control—ego and superego controls. In the students we have just talked about, overcontrol of impulse inhibits development. There are other students who find societal expectations and norms no longer adequate or who have abrogated some past inner constraints upon the expression of artistic, intellectual, sexual, or other inclinations. But they have not found their way as yet to integrating their impulse life in such a manner as to allow for a cumulative and productive development of their potential and for relations with other people that are at once autonomous and interacting. They may be drifting from subject to subject or situation to situation. This drift can be characteristic of the experimentation of adolescence. But in some students it goes deeper and may remain a more permanent characteristic of the personality, somewhat hidden by the adoption of social roles and manners that gloss over the basic uncertainty and lack of a firm center of personality.

The student who may be termed a "good developer" is characterized by increasing freedom of expression and at the same time by more sophisticated forms of control exhibited in emotional and cognitive competencies. This student allows himself self-awareness, engages in self-scrutiny, does not need to gloss over failures or hostile and destructive tendencies in himself and in others, and does not need to get embarrassed over tender emotions and feelings. He has a good grasp of the impact of environmental factors upon him. He will not resort to self-blame when environmental factors are strong determinants. He can distinguish between what is inside and outside of himself and set in motion activities that lead to a change of the external situation either by removing himself from or changing a confining context. He is capable of taking risks.

He realizes that the consequences of an action, such as changing a major, leaving a school, or exposing himself to the possibility of social sanctions have consequences for his inner development and his standing in society which he cannot foresee and yet he feels that what is moving inside of him can achieve definition only by being expressed in some sort of action. While his decision making often is accompanied by anxiety and uncertainty, after the decision, a special kind of calm, sense of achievement, and even exultation prevail.

Students whose development is in the direction just described tend to come from families in which the members could express their differing views and be heard without undue rejection, suppression, or ridicule. Respect for difference and for individuality were marked. When parents exercised authority, there was less blurring between parental judgment and the point of view and feeling out of which the child had made a contrary attempt. The saying that something is demanded for the child's "own good" may tend to a simultaneous overpowering of the child's will, judgment, and action. Respect for difference within the family seems an important means towards developing differentiation of the personality.

We have distinguished different patterns of psychological change in college students. Whatever the personality structure, psychological development is a slow process. The task of achieving greater emotional security, adequate social and sexual roles, and autonomous competencies are so complex and often so beset by trial, error, and anxiety that the developmental psychologist at times finds himself at odds with other people's expectations of what may be accomplished in four years. The psychosocial tasks of adolescence are overwhelming in themselves. To them are added the academic tasks of comprehensive mastery of some of the accumulated knowledge of our cultural and scientific past and present. The time thus needed for growth and differentiation has led Kenneth Keniston (1970) to suggest that we designate a stage between adolescence and adulthood which he calls the state of "youth" and which terminates differently for different individuals, around age thirty. But while development can be a slow process, it needs to be kept in mind that the college environment and the society often exert their own retarding and inhibiting influences.

ADOLESCENTS' UTILITY FOR SOCIETY

Many descriptions of adolescence, by laymen and scientists alike, are couched in pathological terms. There is a singling out of their rebelliousness, their desires for instant betterment, their lack of tolerance, their rationalizations, their romantic idealism, and so on. Yet to think of adolescence as a temporary tumultuous aberration is to do injustice not just to the adolescent's self-concept but to the peculiar potentialities of that stage in life. There is, as we have indicated, a direction toward growth in much of what he does. The adolescent's rebelliousness often is a quite acute critique of the shortcomings of institutions and adult behavior. The adolescent's demand for action is not necessarily an incapacity to tolerate delay but a challenge to the procrastinating delays of adults, their settling into half-painful and half-deadening routines. The adolescent's demands for societal changes are not necessarily a lack of realism but rather an unwillingness to accept certain conventional definitions of "reality." His articulations may not be fully clear or technically sophisticated— though with encouragement students have drawn up highly complex critiques and plans of action—but they often point to the soft spots of our reality. Adults often have concentrated on the style or incompleteness of adolescent expression and have missed the message; they have corrected the spelling and neglected the idea.

Adolescence is a socially very useful stage. Because young people do not yet have a commitment to society as it is, do not yet have obligations of family and occupation, and are characterized by very flexible psychological dispositions, they are, as we have indicated at the beginning of this paper, eminently at a stage in life in which self-renewal, a development of the person toward greater expression of potential and mastery of the environment, is possible. This can enable them, especially in times of rapid change, to be oriented toward the future (some of which is already here) and to be the group that can help society both to recognize and to cope with the new conditions it is facing. In the early parts of this century we experienced a strong intellectual and pedagogical push towards the discovery of the child: what we can learn from the child, his fresher reflection of life, his emotional directness and honesty. Before us still is the discovery of the adolescent: his critiques of society, the utilization of his energies for refashioning some of the ways in which we behave in regard to each other and the ways in which we organize our work and leisure. Students since the early 1960's have been asking for such a role; thus far society has largely denied it to them.

Adolescence in our society is a time of peculiar bondage. People are at the period in life of maximum energy. Their physical strength is great, their intellectual apparatuses and their capacities for action have reached a high point. Yet we deny them an adequate outlet for their energies, herd them into often huge classrooms, and ask them to sit still so that they may acquire the skills that will mean action *later*. This does almost intolerable violence to the young. We might respond by allowing adolescents to do socially useful work, by giving them a greater share in decision making, particularly as it will affect the future in which they will live. This might mean that periods of work and of intellectual or artistic concentration (school) would alternate, though at no time should work or action and intellectual reflection upon them be greatly segregated.

The student activism that emerged in the 1960's points to new ways of using psychological potential. The personality profiles of student activists (Axelrod, *et al.*, 1969) show high scores on many dimensions that educators would find desirable. Activists tend to score high on capacity for awareness, flexibility, responsiveness to others, imagination, willingness for commitment, and ability to confront social reality in a nonpassive way. The organizational expertise of many activists, which included at times providing supplies, means of communications, instruction, and recreation for large numbers of people, showed the competencies that students could activate once they faced tasks they considered socially and personally useful.

In their reform activities, students could take initiative. Instead of being dictated to or having their activities determined by somebody else's predilections, as is often the case in the classroom, they were in charge and could assert and develop their own autonomy. Activism also generated a strong sense of community. Students were united by common goals, by joint deliberations, by informal ties, by intimate conversation. In contrast to the comradeship and affectionate closeness developed during the pursuit of a common cause, the traditional relations among people in dormitory and classroom seemed distant and impersonal. The loneliness and the depression suffered by many students even under the most favorable residential conditions were temporarily suspended in the activist endeavor.

A psychological reading of student activism reinforces lessons learned from the study of student development. They can be summed up by stating some major conditions for successful development during the college years. These are: (1) facilitation of autonomy, of having a role in determining the situations and actions that affect one's life; (2) opportunity to engage in actions that are useful to other people and useful to oneself; (3) opportunity to produce work that results from the assertion or development of a competence and that is, to oneself, a satisfactory expression of oneself; (4) learning to act in concert with other people so that one's own perceptions become enhanced by being shared and developed with others and one's own capacities are developed through responsiveness to other people's needs and their responses to us.

As one looks at the recent history of student activism, one may come to think that, far from being a disturbing social disruption, it was an expression of profound psychological needs of young people, an attempt at individual and social health rather than troublemaking. There was in the 1960's a great readiness on the part of young people to develop and to educate themselves. But adults largely misread the signs and reacted punitively. A historical moment was lost because of the failure of adult awareness and leadership. Now it remains for those of us who can act in cognizance of psychological knowledge to try, more slowly and more painfully, to refashion our understanding and our response to young people so that institutions may become instrumental in developing people rather than processing them for a society that shows too much dullness and docility on the one side and brute explosiveness, anxiety, and intolerance on the other.

REFERENCES

American Council on Education, Office of Research. *The American Freshman.* Washington, D.C.: American Council on Education, Research Reports, Volume 6, 1971.

Axelrod, J., Freedman, M., Hatch, W., Katz, J., & Sanford, N. *The search for relevance.* San Francisco: Jossey-Bass, 1969.

Blos, P. *On adolescence—A psychoanalytic interpretation.* New York: Free Press, 1962.

Erikson, E. H. Identity and the life cycle. *Psychological Issues,* 1959, *1,* 1–171.

Feldman, K. A., & Newcomb, T. M. *The impact of college on students.* San Francisco: Jossey-Bass, 1969.

Group for the Advancement of Psychiatry. *Sex and the college student.* New York: Atheneum, 1965.

Katz, J., & associates. *No time for youth.* San Francisco: Jossey-Bass, 1968.

Katz, J., Korn, H., Leland, C., & Levin, M. *Class, character, and career.* Stanford, California: Institute for the Study of Human Problems, 1969. Available from Clearinghouse for Federal Scientific and Technical Information, Springfield, Virginia.

Katz, J. *Women and men: New roles and relationships,* 1972 (mimeo). Based on data from the Student Environment Study at Stanford University, 1969–71 and questionnaire data collected at four additional institutions in 1971.

Keniston, K. Youth: A new stage of life. *American Scholar,* 1970, *39,* 631–654.

Korn, H. A. Personality scale changes from the freshman year to the senior year. In Joseph Katz & associates, *No time for youth.* San Francisco: Jossey-Bass, 1968.

Newcomb, T. M., *et al. Persistence and change: Bennington College and its students after twenty-five years.* New York: Wiley, 1967.

Perry, W. *Forms of ethical and intellectual development in the college years.* New York: Holt, Rinehart & Winston, 1970.

Sanford, N. (Ed.). Personality development during the college years. *Journal of Social Issues,* 1956, *12,* 1–71.

Sanford, N. Developmental status of the entering freshman. In N. Sanford (Ed.), *The American college.* New York: Wiley, 1962.

White, R. W. *Lives in progress.* New York: Holt, Rinehart & Winston, 1966.

Additional research literature on personality development during college:

Chickering, A. *Education and identity.* San Francisco: Jossey-Bass, 1969.

Heath, D. H. *Growing up in college.* San Francisco: Jossey-Bass, 1968.

Madison, P. *Personality development in college.* Reading, Mass.: Addison-Wesley, 1969.

3. The Black Student on the College Campus

An Illustrative Case of the Live Blues and Living Color

THOMAS L. WINDHAM

> In the beginning was the deed
> And the deed was death[1]

And the opportunity structure opened. And America not only announced the beginning of an historical epoch, she acted as if it were hers. As if she hypnotized Rosa Parks and forced her to stay in her seat when, quiet as it's kept, what people saw was the loss of hypnotist's power. As if she mesmerized Dr. King and introduced him, not only to his keen sense of justice but also insisted that he express these beliefs in the genius of a dialect which was his, through the brilliance of a strategy which was his, and at the expense of a life which was his which is the price black people in America pay for being mesmerized no more. As if it were she who brought about the heightening sense of consciousness which, though it brought us to the streets, lunchcounters, bus stations and court houses,

[1]Giovanni, Nikki. *Black Feeling, Black Talk, Black Judgment,* "The Great Pax Whitie," New York: William Morrow & Co., Inc., 1970, p. 62.

77

was really the resurrected thoughts of my great great grandfather, my great grandfather, his children, and his children's children 'cause while America acted as she did, as she does, taking the credit from us and assigning it to the residents of her liberal belt, she at the same time behaved as if these times were an historical period. She ignored the crux of our position and created and passed laws which had already been created and passed several times years and years ago.

The media, pseudo-historians, sociologists, and politicians reverently announced a new decade of progress. Americans, wanting to believe their message, were forced to believe it, not knowing or attending to the fact that the most powerful factor of this coercion was their wanting to believe it. And one reason for their wanting to believe it was the planted content which had been presented to them since their emergence from the womb, content asserting that liberty and justice for all is a fact. The acceptance of this assertion as fact coerced the beliefs in the new announcement of progress for it was consonant with the preexisting misconceptions which composed the structure of their cognitive categories. And some Americans didn't want to hear it so they continued to refer openly to us as a bunch of communist-inspired niggers, but most people, in spite of the warning of Malik Shabazz and Bobby Seale and the death of Kennedy, said, "Things are getting better . . ." and believed it.

The occupational opportunities for many of America's African population were substantially augmented. Some mothers could stop wondering, for a little while anyway, whether their child would spend a significant period of his youth in jail, waste his life in the employment structure of the gutter, be the subject of the military's game: pin the tail on the nigger and if he hollers, bust him; if he don't holler, offer him a stripe; and if he tails his brother, promote him but see to it that he doesn't get above sergeant; or, as a civilian, fade away in the sorting room of the United States Postal Service. The civil rights movement had once more come to fruition—making it necessary for America to adopt a posture which would give her the image of a nation negating apartheid. The voice of the slave had to be silenced. And so it came to pass that business and industry presented themselves as equal opportunity employers. The people looked at the appearance and saw that it was good. It had to be. It was consonant with the expectations derived from the content of their cognitive categories. It enabled the neutralization if not negation of the voices which, via their continued statements concerning the existence of slavery in America, threatened to evoke cognitive dissonance, for "honor is a happy slave."[2]

Slavery requires that its institutions provide the prerequisite for the maintenance of the structure of social order which is conducive to its own ends. One such requirement is the insistence that black people, even black people from the alleged lower class, participate in this structure in such roles as generate the appearance of increased self-esteem. Black teenagers the country wide began to fill out those sheets of paper which hardly made any sense in order to become students of America's institutions of higher education. The most confusing of these forms is the one for financial assistance. Not only is it confusing, it is embarrassing in that people who possess erroneous conceptions about the structure of our families attempt to determine how much money, we, as a family unit, need to survive. The insult of this form is usually a gross overestimation of how much money our parents can comfortably afford to contribute to our higher education. So many of us, while on the campus, either suffer denial or develop guilt feelings for receiving money which was initially planned to be used for little brother's school shoes, grandma's long-planned trip down south, or just plain old family recreation which is an essential for slave families in America. But, at that moment, denial really

[2]Ibid., p. 61.

doesn't matter and guilt is soon overcome because the expectations held both for you and by you made such sacrifices almost pleasurable.

And expectations are too important to be taken lightly. Black college students are too often seen as the beginning. How many know the suffering involved in being the first? Yet here we are, the first of a long line of stolen people to attend one of America's institutions of higher education. And just what is expected of us? What is expected by us? For the most part it is expected that we will be "ideal" students, ladies and gentlemen, who in appreciating the opportunity "given" our people will acquiesce to the panorama of contempt leaking from the doors of the ivory towers. It is expected that we would lose whatever identity we had as black people which hadn't been stolen or forbidden on our earlier voyages. These expectations are manifested in the lack of personnel, black personnel, occupying positions on the campus from which they could encourage and support our developing, or reacquiring and then developing, the lost stolen and reacquired-for-real genotypic behaviors. Who would polish us with positive reinforcement for acquiring skills necessary for the building of nations? Who would help us extinguish our long learned patterns of behavior which is the kingdom of negrodom? Who would be a leaning post when we were falling down and encourage us to keep on pushing when our thing was for real? Who would just call us honey, or pumpkin or puddin' or Jihad or Voodoo or Kuntu . . . or say or do something which would help us feel like being ourselves again? Instead, we receive the greetings of a dried-up official who tells us that all of us won't make it. Imagine—here you are, the hope, during the first week of school and the Dean or some official representative of that institution enters in his freshly ironed gabardine suit, and wrinkled shirt, or if he's . . . anyway . . . in his imported dashiki wearing a well-rounded 'fro, smites Sly and tells you that very few of you will make it. And if

Pygmalion ever lived she's alive and well at America's institutes of higher education.

At home there was a subtle atmosphere of pride which when contaminated with justified fear and anxiety expressed itself in situations where family members, which of course included the sister upstairs who because her children didn't go to college adopted you and like your mother she was often seen getting off the subway or bus at four o'clock each week-day under the protection of a rayon kerchief, carrying two brown paper shopping bags . . . one inside the other, sporting the walk of a tired sister supported by two barking dogs announcing the end of another day of days work which testified to the real structure of employment opportunities. Finally reaching the bench in front of her project building or the house of a neighborfriend her first real conversation of the day would begin and in it would be announced your acceptance to college.

"Haven't seen Butch around this month, have ya? No— he's away at school, goin' to college now."

. . . 'cause you were strong enough, pushed enough, or crazy enough to go.

"He's gonna make somethin' of himself."

And since you know that's what everyone expects, you decide to stay at the institute of higher education and despite that arrogant soothsayer of a dean or school official, get a degree.

Expectations were great.

Black people were perceived as having a future in America and America boasted of liberty and justice for all. And while folks were getting fire-hosed, attacked by dogs, bombed, shot, lynched, and imprisoned, black college students wrestled with it all, trying to deal with the role of carrying the white boys' burden while this system insisted on new roles for people who were of African descent. And college had to be an extension of the "majority" American socialization process. And that meant the labeling of us as a minority. The plan was Save America—remember? So while the country was dubbed "the great society" black students were introduced to a new act in hell's theatre of the plantation. We were once again confronted with that language thing, the English language—whatever that is. Trying not to say dis 'n dat we became very conscious of the "poor" speech used at home. Socialization required deracialization and this process begins and ends with language. Language is a mode of thought. One apprehends the universe through language. To take on a language is to take on a culture ... and the assassination of Nommo is the transformation of honey, pumpkin, Jihad, Voodoo, and Kuntu to Mayotte Capecia and Jean Veneuse.

To take on the culture of the "majority" we necessarily reject our own or whatever is left of it. And that's just it. There's so little left because its existence is incompatible with the beliefs and behavioral patterns of the corporate state and the mythology from which they are derived. When our customs were intact, we revolted against that form of existence forced upon us while residing in the new world. We were permitted no legal language, no legal marriage, no legal family, no legal control over our children. We were divided as a function of overexposure to the house and field. And whether from the mouths of Zachary and his financiers, apologists, or abolitionists, we were both presented and perceived as culturally, biologically, and intellectually inferior. And knowing that stereotypes mediate the perception of reality we know that we have to out-perform white students 'cause when we don't we'll get C's which stand for colored and when we do they'll still get A's. Wanting to make it, wanting to and hoping to respond to the dreams of great great grandfathers and the children of their children's children we carry on.

Some joined the debate team, and while acquiring valuable skills, were informed that while attending tournaments in certain States we'd have to lodge in separate quarters. And we carried on, hoping to learn something

which would be beneficial to our community and suddenly coming to the realization that nowhere in the plans
made for us by "our" schools is there the least shred of
anything which might lead us to even suspect that we
have a community either back home or right in this college town and here on this college campus. Hoping to
learn something which we could use at home we shrink,
scream, and don't give a damn before "professors" whose
mentality is as good an ambassador of this Manichean
universe as is the physical appearance of the man from
Glad. Mythologists addressing themselves to the use of
the word black by the Romans and Greeks. Psychologists
addressing themselves to white rats and white college
sophomores. We continue to go to class because we knew
that being the one or one of two or possibly three black
students in the class we'd be missed. We sometimes
refused to attend class 'cause there are days when we are
unable to accept the history of Europe as the history of the
world and refuse to believe that the history of America
began with some dude called Columbus. In complete ig-
norance of Nkrumah and DuBois and believing the
United Fruit Company to be an example of free enter-
prise, professors tell us of their wish for more negroes at
their institutions. And I'm sure such expression was a firm
belief. They NEEDS negroes and IS very fond of Afro-
Americans. But what does that term mean in a nation
whose countrymen believe that Africa is the dark continent where savages sprint through infected jungles in
search of Tarzan? Look at contemporary politics while
not forgetting its Manichean structure and what does it
mean? It means tension. How can we be both African and
American without being under tension? The term Afro-
American, like many terms manifesting the misguided
genius of Yankee ingenuity, collapses two antithetical
concepts and cloaks the nucleus of our protest. We've
never been Americans and have not been permitted to
practice our being as Africans. So we hang in the imbal-

ance and are forced to be an accomplice to this mode of existence . . . and then we are presented to ourselves and the world as minorities.

Signified.

Stares . . . glares . . . hardened glances. Away from home. Discovering the stares of white students and university personnel aren't particularly dismantling since they are so much like those we see when, for one reason or another, we find ourselves out in the suburbs after working hours, or in a museum attempting to reconcile and even understand the artifacts of a strange culture which has been and is being presented as superior to the cultures of Africa, Asia, and Latin America. What is significant about these stares is the fact that they belong to your classmates, roommates, neighbors, maids, maintenance men, teachers, regents, dieticians, kitchen help, etc. who are now members of one's immediate environment, immediately informing us that the gaze of the other is now there to haunt us in those places and during those activities which used to be private in the special sense that if others were present they were like you and their presence, rather than eliciting a consciousness permeated with object-like existence, let you in most instances act like youself. Saucer eyes didn't confront you at the dinner table, raising questions about your liberal use of pepper and your habit of folding your bread. Back home Caucasian ladies weren't present in situations where they would let you know that they wanted to touch your hair while knowing all along, as white people know about black people, that if you cut it off and saved it, the money budgeted for brillo would no longer be necessary. And suddenly you understand why Mamas pressed their hair and Daddies came home high on Friday nights.

Though while downtown we were always watched and suspected of being thieves by nature of genetics we didn't have to wonder why our neighbors hid their valuables, which really aren't valuable anyway, from us because that hardly happened. And when it did it was because we were in the home of a misguided brother who internalized the dominant culture's stereotypes of us. For us survival was structured around the sharing of flour and cheese which was obtained from a bureau alleged to be the Department of Public Welfare, selling porgies for a nickel so we could go back to the water and get more porgies and enjoy both fishing and bringing fish back to the block, telling the number man that the police had been asking for him and figuring out a hip way to trip that white lady who dressed in blue and calling herself a public health nurse possessed a culturally acquired proclivity for embarrassing and humiliating our parents. And though we often argued and fought we never had to justify our warm greetings, pretty-colored clothes, and Louisiana Hot Sauce. Even though we played the dozens, sounding on each other, each other's mamas and daddies and any other thing that one could sound on, we never SNUCK in an occupied bathroom or peeked into a shower stall to see if our genitals reached our knees.

Stress?

Stigmatized.

Defined and overdetermined . . . from without.

So we form Black Student Unions because we realize that we are politically, socially, and economically disenfranchised on the campus. We request black or third world dormitories. While white students live in white fraternity houses and mostly white dorms we are informed by both the courts and the schools that our request is unconstitutional. And we learn that the relationship between our BSU's and the institution at large is one which only cloaks our dependency on the school. Some of us keep on pushing. Some of us land in jail . . . because of it. Some of us, via one of the many ways of withdrawing from school, withdraw or are withdrawn. Some of us internalize the socialization process, get a Degree and work at the front office of an equal opportunity employer . . . enabling the nation to continue to believe in its generous response to our movement, not understanding what we are all about. What we've been talking, marching, sitting, and fighting about is not the show-and-tell job in front of some picture window but the master-slave relationship. Sisters still gettin' off the trains and busses at four o'clock protected by a rayon kerchief; carrying two brown paper shopping bags one inside the other, sporting the walk of a tired woman supported by barking dogs announcing the end of another day of days work, finally reaching the bench in front of her project building or the house of a neighborfriend to begin her first real conversation of the day and in it she announces that you are away at college. And you, knowing that you have to go, while WE make that thing of life, releasing the Blues and reviving Muntu, that thing which in a special sense already is and will become, try to ignore the stares, glares, misconceptions, and distortions. History has not ended . . . despite the fact that Afro-Americans AND black people leave places like IBM at five o'clock with dogs that don't bark. And now it's "rumored" that our numbers of America's institutions of HIGHER EDUCATION ARE DWINDLING! . . .

4. Can Biology Help Explain the Revolt of Youth?

ROBERT DEBRÉ

The following paper is the only one in this volume which has a previous publication history. It appeared originally (in French) in the December, 1969 issue of Revue de Paris *under the title, "La Biologie Aide-t-elle à Comprendre la Jeunesse Révoltée?" The paper has been translated and appears here because, first, it presents an important perspective on issues related to student stress in the campus community, and second, it has had an enormous influence on current international research activity in the field of campus stress, having played a seminal role in the development of the international study on the biological aspects of student unrest. As the reader will note, the term "biological" is used very broadly, virtually synonymous with "conditions of life."*

Professor Debré, born in 1882, has had a distinguished career in virology, clinical bacteriology, infant and child health care, and adolescent medicine, and his name is associated with fundamental research in childhood tuberculosis, infant nutrition, the discovery of streptomycine, the identification of tubercular meningitis, the prevention of rubeola and diphtheria, the identification of certain forms of diabetes, kidney and thyroid diseases,

87

and the involvement of molecular biochemistry in the development of congenital malformations. His work has been instrumental in the development of child health service programs in France. His work and thought has earned him a place of honor in 20th Century French medicine and social ideology.

In spite of the fact that so many studies have already appeared regarding the youth revolt, perhaps a physician whose work has been devoted to studying youth may venture to offer some ideas concerning this movement which has shaken the world's universities, and even threatened the stability of certain governments. May he be permitted to speak as a biologist not accustomed to separating man's emotions, thoughts, actions and words from his total being? With such a point of view one sees but one particular aspect of the serious problem which concerns us. But perhaps we can attempt to clarify some aspects of this widespread condition and propose some suggestions based upon our analysis of this profound, generalized and probably long-lasting situation.

The trouble of which we speak has affected youth at a clearly defined period in its life and development; this period extends from about the 15th year until adulthood, which is believed to begin at the time an individual stops growing in height, that is to say—we shall return to this point—between the 20th and 25th years.

A well-known basic fact, one which should be emphasized from the start, is the world-wide character of the revolt among university students. It would not be fair to pass judgment on the origins of this movement by only taking into account the situation in one particular country and by reviewing only local causes, whether economic, political or intellectual. The fault would be the same as if a physician, in attempting to understand a disease in one country, were to blind himself to its spread throughout the world.

The first point, then, which we should investigate, is the universal character of university disturbances. One might assume either that it is an epidemic which spreads from a primary focus, or else that situations have arisen simultaneously in many parts of the world.

Moreover, even in the case of a contagious disease, dissemination cannot become widespread unless host conditions are favorable. In this instance, we are led to ask ourselves if general conditions have not been established which have suddenly become favorable for the simultaneous appearance of these movements. Present means of communication permit the propagation of ideas, of examples, of forces among human groups in ways completely different from any known previously. Such communication, of course, may encourage a repetition of the same behavior. But the general character of this phenomenon appearing under such diverse social, moral and political conditions, excludes the possibility of any central policy being propagated. And even this call would not have been able to find a sympathetic response had not university youth been ready to listen to it. There is hardly a country which has been spared. If, in some universities, a violent upheaval has not occurred, we have good reasons for believing that political and police oppression may have prevented any public manifestation of the problem which they too experienced. Why have troubles burst forth in universities in New York, Madrid, Tokyo, Paris, Boston, Dakar, Brasilia and Istanbul? Contagion probably played a role, but it would be wiser to suppose that both contagion and similarity of issues and concerns played their part.

Let us examine the special conditions which currently exist in universities, and let us ask whether today's youth differs greatly from those of earlier generations. One thought immediately emerges in considering this problem. There exists a biologic process which affects all youth, particularly in the countries and social classes where living conditions are good. We should like to describe its basic features. It is a well known phenomenon that the human species changes gradually and that one of the most obvious elements of this change is its increase in height—man has grown taller. It is said that a soldier of today would have difficulty fitting into medieval armor. The Norwegian government has data for military recruits covering 200 years. Between 1740 and 1830 no remarkable increase occurred, but between 1830 and 1875 average height increased nearly two inches. A similar trend is in evidence elsewhere in the world—in Japan, Argentina, Esthonia, and the United States. In France the average height of university students has been increasing since the French Revolution. Not only are children and adolescents growing taller, but they are growing more rapidly, and their final growth ceases earlier. At the beginning of the 19th century, human beings reached their ultimate height at 24 or 25 years for boys, and 20 to 22 years for girls. Today this average age has dropped to 19 or even 18 years.

Growth in height, often accompanied by an increase of weight, is not an isolated phenomenon. Development of the human being as a whole is involved. Growth is a metabolic phenomenon which proceeds in orderly fashion and is bound up with the development of the entire organism. Growth results from the totality of all the changes in our tissues, enzymes, hormones, and in the number and volume of our cells. Proof of the importance of this new developmental pace is seen in the earlier appearance of puberty. Thus, in the privileged sector of the great industrial cities of Great Britain, the average female pubertal age in 1820 was 14½ years; today it is under 13 years. The working class, too, has participated in this change, insofar as its living conditions have gradually improved. In the United States, statistics show that since 1900 the age of pubertal onset has fallen continuously. In virtually all countries where data exist, girls, in general, now reach sexual maturity 10 months earlier than did their mothers. There are many reasons for believing that this fact, while more obvious in girls, is common to both sexes, and that the speed of this evolution is accelerating. It is generally accepted that there is a relationship between this acceleration and the improvement in nutrition, hygiene, and general living conditions. Small mutational genetic changes may also modify human characteristics, but it is more likely that better food intake and living conditions allow those who benefit from these improvements to attain the level predetermined by their basic hereditary potential. Poor living conditions, contrariwise, interfere with the achievement of this genetic potential.

Thus, children mature earlier at the very time in history that their school life is being prolonged and their economic and social independence delayed, especially as a result of the continuation of their school studies. Hence, there is a growing contrast between an earlier starting and more rapidly achieved adolescence on the one hand, and an increasing and delayed achievement of manhood —in the social sense of this old word—on the other hand.

The upheavals of the pubertal and postpubertal period induce widespread changes. Ways of feeling, intellectual activities, motives for acting, and total behavior are all changed. Everyone knows the various effects of this crisis. This "psychosomatic" revolution in the developed countries is the opposite of what happens to the people living in the Third World. There children and adolescents grow up later, more slowly, and for a longer period of time, and the onset of sexual maturation does not arrive earlier. In the prosperous countries, and in the more favored social classes of other countries, there is a growing spread between the biological maturation of the individual and his social maturation, if one may use this term. We can, then, understand why the resistance, the drives, particularly sexual, the revolt against the older generation and society, as well as the boundless enthusiasm that characterizes this postpubertal period of life, are strongest among youth, and why the youth movement has so little patience with the steadiness of adults. The striving for freedom is, moreover, ambivalent, for it is accompanied by a need for guidance, which will manifest itself sooner and because of this profound agitation of the total individual.

One must also think of the unhappy consequences of the last World War, which affected the entire world, including the neutral countries. Almost everywhere, children and mothers who were pregnant or were about to become pregnant were subjected, along with the rest of the populace, to poor living conditions. Malnutrition stopped the growth of Parisian children during the years of the occupation. Without doubt these children later "caught up," for the human organism has remarkable recuperative powers. Nevertheless, the human organism, especially when it is young, forgets nothing. The effects of somatic and psychic traumata suffered by the mother can manifest themselves in disturbances in the child. However obscure these factors may be, the findings in man, as well as in experimental animals, underline this aspect of the problem we are studying. The influence of nutrition and the environment during the early postnatal days has serious, fixed and irreversible effects. Granting the obvious correlation between development, especially of the endocrine system, and adolescent behavior, it is not surprising that youth today is both different from the preceding generation, and more deeply disturbed.

It is understandable that this unrest, in the widest sense of the term, is noted in all countries, among students who belong to the privileged classes. As a matter of fact, it is university youth who have been almost exclusively involved. The difficulty is bound up with a change in the entire young generation and the impetus leading to violence has appeared particularly clearly among young intellectuals. The political leanings of some, as well as the generosity peculiar to this age, have led them, here and there, to develop joint efforts with working class youth— since they scarcely have any contact with peasant youth. It is because university youth live under new conditions that uprisings in universities have occurred. Doubtless, the universities have always been turbulent, and the Latin Quarter, for example, has been agitated at numerous times in the past. But at present, the student world has become a very special kind of world. In my youth, we created small groups of students in each field of study. Today, hundreds and thousands enroll in the school of higher education. It is well known that emotional reactions change completely when the individual finds himself at the center of a crowd. Crowds are violent; they attack an obstacle and are themselves destroyed—or they destroy it. The study of animals allows one to apply these group phenomena to other species, including man.

Man, especially the young, is dominated by an aggressive drive when in a mob. Easily angered, crowds damage, destroy, defile, and break. Adolescent groups charge willingly into battle. Would there have been so many wars without this? Totalitarian regimes before World War II were well aware of what they were doing in uniting fascist youth and particularly Hitlerian youth; it was easy to sweep them along towards brutality—indeed in Germany, towards cruelty. Today, the leaders of the Chinese revolution have achieved a new revolution, thanks to organized youth.

In permitting the assembly in universities of thousands of youth—including now a considerable proportion of women—at the exact time of the disturbances under discussion, public authorities run obvious risks. In France, no part of the social structure provides for the existence of similar youth assemblages except the army, where rigor and discipline of young men prevails.

Yet there has been no hesitation in creating university campuses which serve to accentuate the tendency of our students toward a continuous collective life, and more serious still, toward separation from the community. A kind of enclosed field of action has been created where fermentation is favored.

That is not all. Among the young university students, there has occurred a kind of break in equilibrium, related to the fact that their work is almost exclusively intellectual. Sports, even in the Anglo-Saxon countries, interest only a small fraction of them. We mean *participation* in

sports and not simply viewed on television. As a result of
the widespread use of automobiles and motorcycles, the
healthy custom of walking has disappeared. University
youth were formerly poor, but those of today, at least in
most countries, whether from the upper, middle, or lower
bourgeousie, are provided with money and facilities
which free them from many restraints. The overloading
of certain curricula, difficult to avoid because of the
progress in knowledge and the tough competition, results
in excessive intellectual work.

Variety is indispensable for good physiologic balance
and should be achieved during the daily life of the young.
Hygiene and the daily student work schedule, including
that of young teachers, are not good. An accurate recount-
ing of Hellenic culture—during its height—should be accompanied by a plea for a balanced way of life, something
too often forgotten. Physical exercise is neglected, and
manual labor is considered a complete bore. It is not without serious damage that, among many young people, the
thinking man has stamped out the working man.

The biologist must of necessity examine the whole man,
and should study his thinking processes and his influence
on the ideas of those about him. Specifically, the idea of
liberation is extremely important in the world of this
young generation: liberation of women, liberation of social classes, and liberation of peoples is being achieved
under the eyes of a tumultuous youth, oriented towards
its own liberation through the abolition of the religious,
moral, and social restrictions of its elders. Disputes with
parents spread to teachers who, at the same time, are
their judges. Thus it is in opposing the regulations dictated by adults, that these newly aroused forces obtain
their initial stimulus.

If there is some truth in the analysis that we have attempted, it is legitimate to ask the physician, who attempts to arrive at a diagnosis, to prescribe treatment. In
our opinion the reforms should bear less on the curricula,
the degrees, and the examinations (which have often

been modified in haste), than on the life itself of today's student.

First, we have seen that the separation of the university environment from the community is harmful because it favors the gathering together of students who become a prey to unrest, which can stimulate violence. Besides, this separation does not allow students to participate directly in the new industrial and technical revolution which we are experiencing. Second, we have pointed out that many of the young become adults during the period of their studies. Should they not be treated as adults, especially by encouraging them to live as adults?

Third, the equilibrium of students' lives, disturbed by an excess of intellectual work, should be reestablished by incorporating manual work or work as an artisan or artist or laborer into their activities. From such beginnings they could not only educate themselves but they would contribute to national production. Their health—physical and moral—would be better were they to combine the work of hand and brain, and were they to participate simultaneously in the life of the university and that of other social classes. It is on this path that one would find, we believe, one of the means of decreasing the separation of the university from the community. The movement would create a revision of the scale of values in an educational process which would be at once intellectual and technical.

These suggestions would be enhanced if the young of all social classes were admitted to universities in much greater numbers than at present. This act of social justice, which requires delicate handling to be effective, would result in an outpouring of currently misdirected energy and also a university population accustomed to serious work, and having a well-developed sense of altruism. By following these paths, the university would be not only liberal, as it has been and should be, but also liberating.

Part II

RESEARCH AND PROGRAM REVIEWS

5.   Research on College Dropouts

A Critical Look

FRANK R. TIMMONS

Dropping out of college is a complex process which has been investigated for approximately fifty years. Yet it remains little understood. Part of the reason for this lack of understanding lies in the fact that the large majority of studies of dropping out have proceeded without any articulated conceptual framework within which to organize hypotheses and evaluate the significance of findings. The present paper attempts to clarify some of the reasons why development of theoretical understanding of the dropout process has been minimal, despite a considerable accumulation of data (for reviews see Marsh, 1966; Sexton, 1965; Summerskill, 1962; Timmons, 1971). The paper approaches this task first by presenting the minimal requirements that a study must meet in order to contribute results that can add to our base of knowledge. It then focuses on the research articles that meet these criteria, summarizes the state of knowledge with regard to college dropouts, and offers suggestions with regard to future research.

CRITERIA FOR AN ADEQUATE STUDY

I: Definition of Dropout

Approximately 100 empirical articles and 40 case reports and general discussions of college dropouts have appeared in the literature in the last 20 years. In the overwhelming majority of the empirical studies, a dropout has been defined in the broadest sense possible, i.e., as anyone who leaves a college or university in which he is enrolled prior to graduating. Typically, no distinction has been made between students who leave voluntarily and students who leave involuntarily (are dismissed by the institution); nor have students who transfer from their college of original enrollment to another college or university (transfers) been differentiated from students who drop out of their college of original enrollment without transferring (nontransfers). Yet, compelling evidence, which is elaborated later in the present paper, suggests that combining these diverse groups of students leads to confusion and serious distortions in our picture of dropping out (Conner, 1966; Eckland, 1964a, 1964b, 1964c; Hackman & Dysinger, 1970a, 1970b; Max, 1969, Office of Dean of Women, 1960; Stordahl, 1970). Thus, the first requirement for an adequate study of dropouts is the separation of transfers from nontransfers and voluntary withdrawals from involuntary withdrawals.

II: Methodological Issues

A second major shortcoming in most studies of college dropouts is their failure to utilize a comparison or control group. They merely report characteristics of students who drop out, without any evidence that they are significantly different from students who do not drop out. A related deficiency that leads to problems in interpreting results stems from the failure to use large enough samples of subjects to permit statistically reliable results and meaningful interpretation of data. Finally, as in the example below, even when results attain statistical significance, they can lead to misleading conclusions.

To give but one example of this common occurrence, Beahan (1966) administered a questionnaire to all incoming freshmen at one university and found that an affirmative answer to the following question "portended a statistically significant higher likelihood of dropping out of school than a negative answer to this question": "Do you have alternating moods of undue gloom and cheerfulness? [Beahan, 1966, p. 306]." However, upon close examination of his data, it is clear that while the answer to the above question was significantly different for students who dropped out as opposed to students who remained (he did not differentiate between transfers and nontransfers), there were a large number of false negatives and false positives. Of 274 students who answered the question affirmatively, 130 (47 percent) dropped out. Of 2262 students who answered the question negatively, 698 (31 percent) dropped out. Thus, a higher absolute number of dropouts answered this question in the negative and would not have been predicted to leave. Moreover, it would have been predicted incorrectly that an additional 144 students who answered in the affirmative would have dropped out. Thus, even statistically significant results can lead to misleading conclusions and must be interpreted carefully.

From this discussion, three major criteria for an adequate study emerge. They are: (1) a definition of dropping out which separates transfers from nontransfers and voluntary withdrawals from involuntary withdrawals; (2) the use of a comparison or control group; and (3) a large enough sample size, chosen randomly, to permit statistically reliable results, with the caveat that careful interpretation of the results is also required.

If these criteria are met, exploratory work can begin to build a reliable data base while theoretical development is proceeding concurrently. Studies which do not meet these minimal criteria are of questionable value as far as increasing our understanding of the general issue of college dropouts. They may, in fact, lead to confusion.

INCIDENCE OF DROPPING OUT

Ever since Summerskill's (1962) review of dropout research dating from the 1920's through the 1950's, his conclusion regarding the incidence of dropping out has been cited by almost every researcher in the field. He stated that:

> American colleges lose, on the average approximately half their students in the four years after matriculation. Some 40% of college students graduate on schedule and, in addition, approximately 20% graduate at some college, some day. These have been the facts for several decades in American higher education [Summerskill, 1962, p. 631].

He cautioned, however, that variability is high between colleges, that statistical surveys of college dropouts have sometimes been inadequate in their sampling procedures, that attrition rate has been variously defined, and that the data from different studies are difficult to compare.

Although they have usually been ignored, such cautionary statements are very important. In fact, the often-repeated claim that 40 percent of entering college students fail to graduate is highly questionable. Two factors have been primarily responsible for this misleading conclusion. One is that most investigations have neglected to ascertain the whereabouts of students who do not return to their college of original enrollment once they leave it. Typically, college records are examined and if students' names are missing, they are labeled "dropouts." The second factor is the "failure of [most] studies to make adequate allowance for the prolonged nature of

academic careers and the dropouts who [return] [Eck-
land, 1964b, p. 403]."

In a study of freshmen who left the Madison campus of
the University of Wisconsin, Lins and Abell (1966) found
that 68.6 percent of their subjects had received further
formal education in some college or university by the end
of the fourth semester after their original enrollment. The
Office of the Dean of Women at the University of Michigan (1960) and Stordahl (1970) report similar percentages
of transfers. Moreover, Conner (1966) found that *84 percent* of the "dropouts" in his study transferred to another
college or returned to S.M.U. Finally, Cope and Hewitt
(1971) found that within two years, 75 percent of the
"dropouts" in their survey were attending other colleges
and universities. Thus, to call a student a "dropout" because he leaves his college of original enrollment may be
meaningful for the administrative purposes of a particular
institution, but to assume that he is a dropout from higher
education is unwarranted. In fact, longitudinal data especially highlight the distortion that can result from such a
presumption.

Eckland (1964b, 1964c), in a 10-year follow-up investigation that differentiated transfers from nontransfers,
found that only 26.6 percent of the 1180 men in his final
sample graduated in four years from *any* college or university. However, by the end of the follow-up period, 66.3
percent had graduated and an additional 4.5 percent
were seniors who appeared to be potential graduates in
the near future. This rate was obtained for a group of male
freshmen who enrolled in the University of Illinois under
an unrestricted admissions policy, thus suggesting that
the eventual graduation rate for selective colleges might
be even higher.

This speculation is supported by evidence from a study
by Max (1969), which is based on students who entered
the senior colleges of the City University of New York in
1960 as full-time day students. Her data indicate that of
the 7,848 freshmen admitted, 48 percent received de-

grees within four years. By the end of a seven-year follow-up period, 71 percent had received degrees from the college they originally entered as freshmen. Of the students who had not graduated, 2.3 percent were still enrolled in day or evening sessions, 7.1 percent had requested transfers to another college, 8.8 percent had been dismissed because of academic deficiencies or left college while on probation, and 11.3 percent withdrew for other reasons.

In a parallel study on subjects who graduated from their college of original enrollment *or* from another college to which they transferred, Max (1969) found a 79.4 percent graduation rate for 3,246 subjects who originally entered Brooklyn or Queens College as freshmen. Of the students who had not graduated from some college at the end of seven years, 3.1 percent were still enrolled in college, 3.5 percent had not received a degree and were not enrolled, 6.2 percent could not be located, 7.6 percent did not reply to the questionnaire mailed to them, and .3 percent were in other categories. Of the students who transferred from their college of original enrollment, *91 percent* had received degrees.

These figures indicate the extreme importance of making differentiations within the broad category of dropping out and make clear the misleading conclusions that can come from studies that do not. In addition, they point to the need for following students longitudinally if we are to obtain an accurate assessment of actual dropouts from higher education. The following section provides additional documentation of the importance of making distinctions between transfers and nontransfers and between voluntary and involuntary withdrawals.

FACTORS ASSOCIATED WITH DROPPING OUT

In previous reviews of research on college dropouts (Marsh, 1966; Sexton, 1965; Summerskill, 1962; Timmons, 1971), long lists of characteristics of "dropouts" have been presented, with the warning that there are many contradictions in the literature. One approach to trying to make sense of these contradictions has been to talk about students in relation to particular college or university environments and to think of dropping out as the result of a "lack of fit" between the student and the environment at a particular school (Astin, 1964; Chickering, 1969, 1970; Gurin, Newcomb, & Cope, 1968; Panos & Astin, 1968; Pervin & Rubin, 1967; Stern, 1966).

In terms of increasing understanding of person-environment interaction, this area of research is very important. In addition, it may assist particular colleges or universities in their attempt to assess which "types of students" are most suited for their institutions. However, dropouts from higher education—not just from a particular college or university—can be understood better if they are distinguished from students who merely leave one college to enroll in another. Theoretically, it is logical to expect differences between transfers and nontransfers and between voluntary and involuntary withdrawals. The fact that most studies have combined these various groups is likely to account by itself for the major part of the confusion and contradictions in the results obtained to date.

Factors Associated with the Student.   Even with regard to percentile rank in high school, which has been reported consistently to relate to dropping out of college, Eckland (1964b) found that nearly twice as many students in the 80-99th percentile range graduated *in continuous attendance* as did students in the 40-59th percentile range. However,

> in spite of the latter's propensity to drop out of college, the high school rank of dropouts above the 39th percentile did not predict who would return to college and graduate. This variable, so commonly employed in attrition studies, apparently is far more predictive of college dropout than it is of final graduation [Eckland, 1964b, p. 414].

With regard to most of the personality and social factors which have been asserted to relate to dropping out, the majority of studies that report these findings do not meet the criteria required for inclusion in the present paper. There are, however, a few exceptions.

Eckland (1964a), in a review of 24 investigations which examined socioeconomic status (SES) in relation to dropping out and graduation, reports that the studies which were completed at the end of the freshman year found no significant relationships between SES and dropping out. In 11 of 17 studies which were conducted at the end of two to four years, however, significant differences were found—with social class being especially important as a determinant of graduation for students from the lower ranks of their high school classes. SES was relatively unimportant for students who ranked high in their classes, but for students who ranked low and were also low on measures of SES, graduation was unlikely. By contrast, students from higher SES—even the ones who did not do well in high school—were likely to graduate.

In his own study of dropouts from the University of Illinois, Eckland (1964c) found that a composite index of SES had as much predictive power as high school and early college grades and aptitude tests. Family income *per se* was not predictive of eventual graduation, but factors such as educational level of parents were of major importance.

In the area of motivation, two research reports meet the criteria for inclusion in the present paper. In the first one, Trent and Medsker (1968), in a follow-up study of 9778 high school seniors, found that

> persistence in college is basically a function of three factors: (1) the importance undergraduates themselves assign to the completion of a degree, (2) their having decided by the second year of high school or earlier that they would go to college, and (3) the fact that their parents had definitely wanted them to attend [Trent & Medsker, 1968, p. xi].

In the second report, the authors (Hackman & Dysinger, 1970a) tested the hypothesis that "students who enroll in college with a strong commitment to a college education will be more likely to persist through the critical first year of college [when the dropout rate at most colleges is higher than at any other time] than will students who are less committed [Hackman & Dysinger, 1970a, p. 313]."

Questionnaire data were collected at freshman orientation on 1407 students who were enrolled in three midwestern liberal arts colleges and from the parents of 1331 of these students. After one year the students were divided into four groups: (1) persisters; (2) transfers/returnees (the latter being students who reenrolled in the same college they left); (3) voluntary withdrawals; and (4) academic dismissals. Using analysis of variance to test their hypothesis, they found that nine of 16 analyses were significant at or beyond the .05 level of confidence, with persisters generally being highest of the four groups on the questionnaire items considered relevant to commitment—none of which were significantly correlated with several measures of intellectual competence and personal-social adjustment. Moreover, as in Trent and Medsker's (1968) study, the parents of the persisters were significantly more committed to their children getting a college education than were the parents of the students who left.

This evidence suggests that commitment *per se* plays a role in staying in college. Students who voluntarily withdraw may be less committed to obtaining a college degree, even from the date of their entrance, than are students who persist. Transfers/returnees are apparently more committed to getting a college education than voluntary withdrawals (nontransfers) and less committed than the students who persist at their college of original enrollment. Academic dismissals may be as committed as transfers/returnees, but fail to perform adequately enough to stay in college.

These results lend further support to the logical assumption that meaningful data on college dropouts can be obtained by separating transfers from nontransfers and voluntary from involuntary withdrawals. Not to make these differentiations leads to confusing and misleading results about the personal characteristics of dropouts.

Considerable research employing the Omnibus Personality Inventory (1962) suggests that dropouts in good academic standing (voluntary withdrawals) are more intellectually oriented, more autonomous, creative, complex, open to ambiguity, innovative in their thinking, and more anxious than nondropouts (Chickering, 1969; Hannah, 1971; Heist, 1968; Snyder, 1968). However in none of these studies were transfers differentiated from nontransfers; thus, they provide no data relevant to whether or not these students simply did not fit at their colleges of original enrollment or whether they dropped out of higher education in general.

In the area of emotional problems in relation to dropping out, Hackman and Dysinger (1970b) found that students who were dismissed because of academic deficiencies consistently reported more severe problems than voluntary withdrawals, who were next in terms of the number of severe problems they reported. Transfers/returnees reported the fewest number of severe problems—except that transfers reported more dissatisfaction with the college environment than did the other groups of subjects. These results demonstrate the need to differentiate between the subcategories within the general category of "dropout" if we are to obtain a clear picture of dropping out.

Factors Associated with the College or University. Gurin and his colleagues (Gurin *et al.*, 1968) assert that one of the major problems of much of the research on the personality characteristics of college dropouts is that it has not endeavored to discover individual orientations, which might have relevance for different types of institutional settings. However, they note that Stern and his associates (Pace, 1963; Stern, 1960, 1965, 1966; Stern, Stein, &

Bloom, 1956) have found that factor analyses of their two measures—one of student characteristics and the other of institutional characteristics—have yielded different factor structures at the individual and institutional levels. In fact, "Pace has essentially abandoned the attempt to integrate the individual and institutional levels and has turned to an institutional focus and the development of an instrument to measure contrasting institutional environments [Gurin *et al.*, 1968, p. 11]."

The present paper has argued that this approach may provide important data on person-environment interaction, but that it does not deal with the general issue of dropouts from higher education. Nonetheless, since this approach has been the focus of some recent research, which meets the criteria for inclusion in this paper, these studies are reviewed here.

Conner (1966), in a study which utilized Pace's (1963) College and University Environment Scales (CUES) to assess the environment at Southern Methodist University, found no significant differences between dropouts and "retainees" nor between transfers and nontransfers.

In another study which took into account both student and environmental factors, Horner (1970) used the Transactional Analysis of Personality and Environment (Pervin, 1967a, 1967b, 1968; Pervin & Rubin, 1967), an approach which is based on the semantic differential and which is designed to measure person-environment interaction. She selected randomly 100 persisters (students who went straight through four years at the University of Nebraska from 1964–1968) and 100 nonpersisters (students who entered the University of Nebraska in 1964 but were not in continuous attendance to 1968 and had not subsequently reentered the University of Nebraska or transferred to another college or university), all of whom had grade point averages of 2.0 or higher. The persisters and nonpersisters were requested in the spring of 1968 to fill out the Transactional Analysis of Personality and Environment (TAPE). One hundred percent of the persisters completed the TAPE, and from a larger sample of 300 nonpersisters, 87 percent did so. Of these 261 dropouts upon whom data were available, 100 of them were selected for comparison with the 100 persisters.

In reporting her findings relevant to student-college "fit," the author states:

> In concept analysis, mean ratings of 52 adjectival pairs as measured on TAPE yielded differences. Comparison of the Self-College discrepancy scores by the non-persisting female group withdrawing for marital reasons versus other reasons proved different. Persister and non-persister females differed significantly on the Self-Faculty discrepancy scores. Persister and non-persister males were different in the Self-Administration discrepancy scores with the persisters having greater discrepancy. College-Ideal College discrepancy scores differed in comparison of non-persisting females who withdrew for marriage versus other reasons. . . . No differences emerged in the Self-Student discrepancy scores [Horner, 1970, p. 2850-A].

Unfortunately, these findings are very unclear. First, the author does not indicate whether or not the 52 differences were significant—or how many of them significantly differentiated persisters from nonpersisters. Nor does she indicate the total number of adjectival pairs: were there 52 differences out of 52 or out of 200, for example? Second, she offers no clues regarding why she might have found differences (were they significant?) between nonpersisting females who indicated that they withdrew to get married versus females who withdrew for all other reasons she used in the study. Why were not all subjects significantly different on this variable, and why does the author not report how many subjects actually received discrepancy scores that were significant on the Self-College variable?

Third, she does not report her predictions regarding any of the findings. Surely, she did not expect persisting males to report greater discrepancy on the Self-Administration scale than the nonpersisting males. Again, however, the author reports no significance levels.

Cope and Hewitt (1971) used a 20-item questionnaire to attempt to understand the reasons the students in their sample left college. Although they followed up these students and found that 75 percent of them transferred to other colleges and universities, unfortunately they grouped transfers and nontransfers together for their analyses. Analyzing the "dropouts'" responses to the questionnaire, they found that seven factors emerged to account for 62 percent of the variance. The largest single factor, which they labeled "social," accounted for approximately 20 percent of the variance; a second factor, which they labeled "academic," accounted for approximately 11 percent more of the variance. The other factors were made up of one or two items, and accounted for five to eight percent of the variance each.

The authors conclude that "One step is to identify students likely to have social, religious, or academic difficulty; these data can then become meaningful as part of an early warning system [Cope & Hewitt, 1971, p. 51]." However, "disillusionment over a friendship" is one example of what they termed a "social" item. One may ask how the authors would prevent disillusionment over friendship, even if they could predict which students would become disillusioned. They offer no clues about their theory of change for students who become disillusioned. Moreover, they used no comparison subjects, so there is no way of knowing if these "dropouts" became any more disillusioned over friendship than did students who did not drop out.

Panos and Astin (1968), who included transfers in their nondropouts from a sample of 30,506 students from 248 colleges and universities, found that 21 of 36 college-environment variables

were significantly ($p = .05$) associated with the dropout criterion, independently of those student characteristics that were assessed at the time of matricu-
lation. ... The college measures indicate that students are more likely to complete four years if they
attend a college where student peer relationships are
characterized by Cohesiveness, Cooperativeness,
and Independence. Students are more likely to drop
out, on the other hand, if they attend colleges where
there is relatively frequent Informal Dating among
the students. ... In the domain of interpersonal behavior in the peer environment, dropping out is
more likely in colleges where there is frequent use of
automobiles by the students, and ... it is less likely in
colleges where the students frequently participate in
musical and artistic activities, use the library, and—
somewhat surprisingly—are in relatively frequent
conflict with the regulations [Panos & Astin, 1968, p.
66].

Examining variables related to the classroom environment, the authors found that students are less likely to
drop out of colleges in which the classroom environment
is characterized by a high level of personal involvement
on the part of teachers and fellow students, and where
there is a high degree of familiarity between student and
teacher. Students are more likely to drop out if there is a
relatively high level of cheating and if grading practices
are relatively severe.

Regarding variables related to students' perceptions of
the college, they found that colleges that seemed to foster
dropping out tended to be seen by their students as providing considerable opportunity for social activities, freedom to select one's own courses, and as having a
permissive faculty. Colleges that tended to promote persistence were seen as showing a good deal of concern for
the individual student.

Finally, they found that bigness—having to do with the
amount of time students had to spend getting around
campus—was negatively related to persistence and "Se-

verity of Administrative Policies Against Student Aggression is related to dropping out of college, whereas
Severity of Administrative Policies Against Drinking and
Against Cheating are positively related to completing
four years of college [Panos & Astin, 1968, p. 68]."

Out of this array of findings, two patterns of environmental effects emerged: (1) a pattern that related to interpersonal relationships and that suggested a high level of
student competitiveness and informal dating, combined
with limited opportunities for personal involvement with
the faculty, was conducive to dropping out; and (2) a pattern related to administrative issues, which suggested that
severe grading practices, little faculty concern for the
individual student, and considerable freedom in selecting
courses were conducive to dropping out. With regard to
these findings, the authors note that:

> Although the findings concerning environment
> effects are statistically significant, their possible sub-
> stantive significance is questionable because of the
> relatively small size of the coefficients. . . . [In fact,
> they] suggest that the large known differences
> among institutions in attrition rates are a function
> more of differences in their entering students than of
> differences in measurable characteristics of the envi-
> ronment [Panos & Astin, 1968, pp. 68–69].

Similarly, evidence from the research by Gurin and his
colleagues (Gurin *et al.*, 1968) suggests that personality
characteristics can override disjunction between the student and his environment. When disjunction occurs, a
personality orientation that is characterized by avoidant
tendencies may conduce to withdrawal. Another personality orientation, characterized by autoplastic tendencies, may conduce to changing the self when in a
situation of disjunction. On the other hand, an alloplastic
orientation may result in the student in such a position
attempting to modify the environment—rather than leaving or trying to change himself (*cf.* Hartman, 1958; Hirsch

and Keniston, 1970). Finally, a student who has a high tolerance for frustration may be more likely than another student who feels equally discongruent with the college environment to tolerate the discomforts and persist to graduation despite them (*cf.* Feldman & Newcomb, 1970).

PREVENTION OF DROPPING OUT

Chickering (1970), in a thought-provoking discussion of college dropouts, argues that, compared to students who stay in college, students who leave are more

> autonomous, more impulsive, more complex, and less concerned with practical achievement and material success . . . those who stay, and who at entrance were similar to the leavers [in terms of their personality characteristics] change least [during college]. Therefore, the leavers may need to part company early if their development is to move ahead. Their departures for more challenging and fruitful environments are often healthy steps. These students are taking charge of their own existence and development; their initiative should be valued and fostered, not decried and curtailed. . . . [Furthermore,] the most important index of a college's success and social contribution may well be the quality of its dropouts, not the quality of its graduates. If it helps those atypical students who enter near its upper limits to use the experiences which accompany such deviation to clarify their own purposes and potentials, and if it then encourages them to move on to more developmentally fruitful settings, then its contribution both to the individual and to the nation will be substantial. If, on the other hand, it confirms in such students suspicions of their own idiosyncracy, instability, or illness, and if it will neither recognize their condition nor respond to it, then its potential for damage is great [Chickering, 1970, pp. 7–8].

Since there have been a number of attempts to reduce attrition rates, clearly many persons have not agreed with Chickering. However, to date, efforts at preventing dropping out have attained only minimal success. Since, with but one exception, the studies which report these efforts do not distinguish between transfers and nontransfers, they are not reviewed here (see Harvey, 1970, for a brief review). The exception to this tendency is an action research project at the University of Colorado, one objective of which is to reduce the dropout rate there. Bloom (1971), the project director, states:

> The project was designed to accomplish its objectives by providing membership in a group which had psychological, if not physical reality, thus reducing feelings of isolation, by giving members some reference facts with which to compare themselves, thus reducing feelings of uniqueness, by providing an avenue for them to express their reactions to the university, by giving them some intellectual tools by which they might better understand the stresses acting upon them and their reactions to these stresses, by providing formalized opportunities [through completing questionnaires] to think about their own beliefs, and by providing one additional resource person to talk with in the event of some crisis [Bloom, 1971, p. 9].

Preliminary results indicate that of 70 male members of the cohort group, five (7.1 percent) have transferred to another college or university and another five have dropped out without transferring. Of 109 female cohort members, one (.9 percent) has transferred and 15 (13.8 percent) have dropped out without transferring. The totals for males and females are six transfers (3.4 percent) and 20 dropouts (11.2 percent).

In the comparison group of 257 males and 328 females, 29 males (11.3 percent) and 31 females (9.5 percent) transferred; 23 males (8.9 percent) and 49 females (14.9 percent) dropped out. The total number of transfers was 60

(10.3 percent), and the total number of dropouts was 72 (12.3 percent). Although the cohort group had a higher persistence rate than the comparison group, this difference was accounted for by the number transferring rather than the number dropping out of higher education altogether. Moreover, the number of subjects in the subcategories of the cohort group is too small to permit statistical comparisons. Finally, Bloom (1971) cautions that the cohort members volunteered to participate in the research and the effect of not having a random sample of participants is not known.

SUMMARY OF RESEARCH RESULTS

When transfer students are not considered as dropouts from higher education, approximately 66-80 percent of the students who enter American colleges receive degrees within seven to ten years after their initial enrollment. Four years of continuous attendance is not the typical route to a degree, and the assumption that any student who leaves his college of original enrollment is a "dropout" from higher education is in most cases inaccurate. In fact, in one longitudinal study, 91 percent of the transfer students had received degrees by the end of a seven-year follow-up period.

Students who rank in the 80-99th percentile range in their high school graduation classes are nearly twice as likely as students in the 40-59th percentile range to graduate after continuous attendance in college. However, even though students in the 40-59th percentile range tend to leave college at some point before graduation, their probability of obtaining a degree within a 10-year period after initial enrollment is as high as that of students in the 80-99th percentile range.

Socioeconomic status (SES) is relatively unimportant as a determinant of graduation for students who are in the upper ranks of their high school classes. However, students from the lower ranks who are also of low SES are unlikely to graduate. By contrast, students from higher SES—even the ones who do not come from the upper scholastic ranks in high school—are likely to graduate. Rather than family income, the determining factors seem to be the importance that the students and their parents from higher SES attach to obtaining a college degree. Students who have been encouraged by their parents to obtain a degree and who, themselves, are invested strongly in obtaining a degree, have a higher probability of graduating than do their less committed cohorts.

Students who continue at their college of original enrollment have the highest level of commitment to obtaining a college degree; transfers/returnees are more committed than voluntary withdrawals who do not transfer to another college or reenroll at the same institution they left; and academic dismissals are as committed as transfers/returnees, but fail to perform adequately enough to stay in college.

Students who are dismissed because of academic deficiencies report the greatest number of severe problems, and voluntary withdrawals report the next highest number, with the exception that transfers/returnees report more dissatisfaction with the environment of the college from which they leave than do other students who drop out.

Research on the role of the college or university in conducing students to leave a particular institution may be useful to the school involved and may add to our knowledge of person-environment interaction, but it is of questionable value for increasing our understanding of dropouts from higher education. One monumental study involving 30,506 students from 248 colleges and universities, which focused on characteristics of colleges and universities that tend to conduce to persistence, indicates that the dropout rate is lower in institutions in which: (a) student peer relationships are characterized by cohesiveness, cooperation, and independence; (b) students participate frequently in musical and artistic activities, use the library often, and are in relatively frequent conflict with the college regulations; (c) there is a high degree of personal involvement with teachers and fellow students and a high degree of familiarity between faculty and students; (d) there are severe administrative policies against drinking and cheating. The dropout rate is higher in institutions in which there is: (a) frequent informal dating among students; (b) frequent use of automobiles by students; (c) considerable opportunity for social activities; (d) a relatively high level of cheating; (e) severe grading practices; (f) freedom to select one's own courses; (g) a permissive faculty; (h) severe administrative policies against the expression of aggression by students.

However, the magnitude of these correlations was very small, and the authors concluded that environmental effects *per se* contribute little to dropping out. Research from another large-scale study supports this conclusion with the finding that personality characteristics can override the negative press of the environment if motivation is sufficiently high.

Finally, as far as the personal growth of the individual student is concerned, it is a debatable issue as to whether or not particular colleges should try to prevent their students from dropping out. However, even if the prevention of dropping out is judged to be a desirable goal, efforts to date suggest that it may be a difficult one to achieve.

SUGGESTIONS FOR FUTURE RESEARCH

There are numerous questions which remain unanswered, primarily because only a few studies have made differentiations between the subcategories of dropping out and utilized randomly selected samples of experimental and comparison subjects in sufficient numbers to produce reliable data. Knoell (1960, 1964, 1966), in a series of articles, has made many suggestions for research, the majority of which still need investigating. In fact, the thrust of the present paper is to point out that we need information about almost every facet of dropping out, but data which can augment our very slim base of knowledge can only come from investigations which meet the basic definitional and methodological criteria detailed in this review.

REFERENCES

Astin, A. W. Personal and environmental factors associated with college dropouts among high aptitude students. *Journal of Education Psychology*, 1964, *55*, 219–227.

Beahan, L. T. Initial psychiatric interviews and the drop-out rate of college students. *Journal of the American College Health Association*, 1966, *14*, 305–308.

Bloom, B. L. A university freshman preventive intervention program: Report of a pilot project. *Journal of Consulting and Clinical Psychology*, 1971, *37*, 235–242.

Chickering, A. W. *Education and Identity.* San Francisco: Jossey-Bass, 1969.

Chickering, A. W. The impact of colleges on students. Paper presented at the 137th meeting of the American Association for the Advancement of Science, Washington, D.C., December, 1970.

Conner, J. D. The relationship between college environmental press and freshman attrition at Southern Methodist University. *Dissertation Abstracts*, 1966, *27*, 946-A.

Cope, R. G., & Hewitt, R. G. Types of college dropouts: An environmental press approach. *College Student Journal*, 1971, *5*, 46–51.

Eckland, B. K. Social class and college graduation: Some misconceptions corrected. *American Journal of Sociology*, 1964a, *70*, 36–50.

Eckland, B. K. College dropouts who came back. *Harvard Educational Review*, 1964b, *34*, 402–420.

Eckland, B. K. A source of error in college attrition studies. *Sociology of Education*, 1964c, *38*, 60–72.

Feldman, K. A., and Newcomb, T. M. *The impact of college on students.* San Francisco: Jossey-Bass, 1970.

Gurin, G., Newcomb, T., & Cope, R. G. *Characteristics of entering freshmen related to attrition in the literary college of a large state university.* Office of Education, U.S. Department of Health, Education and Welfare Project No. 1938. Ann Arbor, Mich.: Survey Research Center, Institute for Social Research, University of Michigan, 1968.

Hackman, J. R., & Dysinger, W. S. Research notes: Commitment to college as a factor in student attrition. *Sociology of Education*, 1970a, *43*, 311–324.

Hackman, J. R., & Dysinger, W. S. Reactions to college withdrawal. *Journal of Experimental Education*, 1970b, *38*, 23–31.

Hannah, W. Personality differentials between lower division dropouts and stay-ins. *Journal of College Student Personnel*, 1971, *12*, 16–19.

Hartmann, H. *Ego psychology and the problem of adaptation.* International Universities Press, 1958.

Harvey, J. Preventing college dropouts: A review. *Currents '70*, 1970, No. 3 (Nov.), 1–4.

Heist, P. Creative students: College transients. In P. Heist (Ed.), *The creative college student: An unmet challenge.* San Francisco: Jossey-Bass, 1968. Pp. 35–55.

Hirsch, S. J., & Keniston, K. Psychosocial issues in talented college dropouts. *Psychiatry*, 1970, *33*, 1–20.

Horner, D. R. An analysis of persisters and non-persisters at the University of Nebraska. *Dissertation Abstracts International*, 1970, *30* (7-A), 2850.

Knoell, D. Institutional research on retention and with-drawal. In H. T. Sprague (Ed.), *Research on college students.* Berkeley, Calif.: Western Interstate Commission for Higher Education, 1960. Pp. 41–65.

Knoell, D. Needed research on college dropouts. In J. R. Montgomery (Ed.), *Proceedings of the research conference on college dropouts.* U.S. Department of Health, Education and Welfare Cooperative Research Project No. F-065. Knoxville, Tenn.: University of Tennessee, 1964. Pp. 54–83.

Knoell, D. A critical review of research on college dropouts. In L. A. Pervin, L. E. Reik, & W. Dalrymple (Eds.), *The college dropout and the utilization of talent.* Princeton, N.J.: Princeton University Press, 1966. Pp. 63–81.

Lins, L. J., & Abell, A. P. Survey of fall 1963 Madison campus prior to the beginning of third semester after entrance. Madison, Wisc.: Office of Institutional Studies, University of Wisconsin, 1966. Mimeo.

Marsh, L. M. College dropouts: A review. *Personnel and Guidance Journal,* 1966, *44,* 475–481.

Max, P. How many graduate? *College and University,* 1969, *45,* 63–76. Office of the Dean of Women. Voluntary non-returns. University of Michigan, 1960. Mimeo.

Omnibus Personality Inventory: Research Manual. Berkeley: Center for the Study of Higher Education, 1962.

Pace, C. R. *Technical manual (1963): College and University Environment Scales.* Princeton, N.J.: Educational Testing Service, 1963.

Panos, R. J., & Astin, A. W. Attrition among college students. *American Educational Research Journal,* 1968, *5,* 57–72.

Pervin, L. A. A twenty-college study of student X college interaction using TAPE (transactional analysis of personality and environment): Rationale, reliability, and validity. *Journal of Educational Psychology*, 1967a, *58*, 290–302.

Pervin, L. A. Satisfaction and perceived self-environment similarity: A semantic differential study of student-college interaction. *Journal of Personality*, 1967b, *35*, 625–634.

Pervin, L. A. Performance and satisfaction as a function of individual-environment fit. *Psychological Bulletin*, 1968, *69*, 56–68.

Pervin, L. A., & Rubin, D. B. Student dissatisfaction with college and the college dropout: A transactional approach. *Journal of Social Psychology*, 1967, *72*, 285–295.

Sexton, V. S. Factors contributing to attrition in college populations: Twenty-five years of research. *Journal of General Psychology*, 1965, *72*, 301–326.

Snyder, B. R. The education of creative science students. In P. Heist (Ed.), *The creative college student: An unmet challenge.* San Francisco: Jossey-Bass, 1968. Pp. 56–70.

Stern, G. G, Student values and their relationship to the college environment. In H. T. Sprague (Ed.), *Research on College Students.* Berkeley: Western Interstate Commission for Higher Education and Center for Higher Education, 1960. Pp. 67–104.

Stern, G. G. Student ecology and the college environment. *Journal of Medical Education*, 1965, *40*, 132–154.

Stern, G. G. *Studies of college environments.* Cooperative Research Project No. 378. U.S. Office of Education, 1966.

Stern, G. G., Stein, M. I., & Bloom, B. S. *Methods in personality assessment.* Glencoe, Ill.: Free Press, 1956.

Stordahl, K. Influences on voluntary withdrawal from college. *College and University*, 1970, *45*, 163–171.

Summerskill, J. Dropouts from college. In N. Sanford (Ed.), *The American college.* New York: Wiley, 1962. Pp. 627–657.

Timmons, F. R. The college dropout: A review of empirical and theoretical literature and the presentation of a conceptual framework. Unpublished specialty paper, University of Colorado, 1971.

Trent, J. W., & Medsker, L. *Beyond high school: A psychological study of 10,000 high school graduates.* San Francisco: Jossey-Bass, 1968.

6. Help-Seeking in the College Student: Strength or Weakness?

THOMAS G. CARSKADON

There is considerable question as to what characterizes the college student who seeks help for personal problems while at school, as compared to the student who does not. Is he a maladjusted, anxiety-ridden casualty who staggers through the door, desperate for help, too weak to make it in the college system on his own? Or is he a thoughtful, questioning person who eschews simpler, more established ways of adjusting and has the strength to confront himself and his college environment critically in an attempt at growth? Is he partly each, somewhere between those two poles? The question of what differentiates the helpseeker from the nonhelpseeker is important not only in understanding the nature and needs of the students who are seen at college mental health facilities, but also those of students currently not being reached by such services. Are the helpseekers reflecting relative strength or weakness compared to the nonhelpseekers? Are the most difficult student problems still out there somewhere, untouched by mental health services?

This paper will summarize and discuss the methods and findings of sixteen recent studies comparing helpseekers and nonhelpseekers in a college setting. These include all studies found by the author that directly compare help-seekers and nonhelpseekers at a North American college or university.

EPIDEMIOLOGY OF HELPSEEKING

There have been numerous studies of mental health treatment rates in college settings. Percentages of students seeking help at college mental health facilities vary considerably depending on the college and the availability of facilities. Generally, helpseekers tend to comprise from two to 25 percent of the student population, with five to ten percent being the usual range (Baker, 1965; Reifler & Liptzin, 1969; Coons, 1970; Reifler, 1971). Figures for those thought to need help vary, depending on criteria used, but most commonly are about twice the number of those that seek it (Baker, 1965). Recent reviews and summaries of epidemiological studies have been published by Baker (1965), Segal (1966), Reifler and Liptzin (1969), Coons (1970), and Reifler (1971).

METHODOLOGY OF STUDIES

In comparing helpseeking and nonhelpseeking college students, Davie (1958) used questionnaires, adjective checklists, and factual data to compare students who were and were not seen at the mental hygiene division during their undergraduate years at Yale University. Rust (1960) administered a twelve-problem scale to Yale students and assessed its relationship to the probability of students consulting the mental hygiene clinic. Braaten and Darling (1961) were able to compare users of the Cornell mental health division with the general student population on several factual variables. Weiss *et al.* (1965), Segal *et al.* (1966), and King (1967) gave the MMPI to Dartmouth College students and compared the psychiatric utilization rates of those with and without high scores on the MMPI.

Also at Dartmouth, Segal *et al.* (1965) gave the MMPI to all freshmen, and, controlling the variable of adjustment as evidenced by that test, examined psychiatric utilization rates in relation to social variables. Boyce and Barnes (1966) at the University of Western Ontario compared student users and nonusers of university psychiatric facilities on a number of variables. Later Boyce and Thurlow (1969) made another study of users and nonusers of university psychiatric and counseling facilities. Scheff (1966) gave a problem checklist to student users and nonusers of the psychiatric clinic of the University of Wisconsin, and, with the problem variable controlled, compared the two groups. At Wisconsin, Linn (1967) compared applicants for counseling at a psychiatric outpatient clinic with the general student population. Reifler, Liptzin, and Fox (1967) compared users of the psychiatric section of the student health services of the University of North Carolina with the general student population on several variables. King (1968) used extensive data on two undergraduate classes at Harvard College to compare those who did and did not seek psychiatric help from any source during their undergraduate years. At MIT, Snyder and Kahne (1969) compared undergraduate student users and nonusers of the psychiatric services there on Omnibus Personality Inventory scores and some other variables. Walters (1970) compared students visiting the mental health division of the University of Illinois with the general student population on several factual variables. Finally, West (1971) used several subjective measures on sophomore students on academic probation at the University of Rochester to compare users and nonusers of a university counseling facility.

It can be seen that studies relevant to helpseeking behavior in college students tend to be one or a combination of three types. The epidemiological type describes treatment rates and estimates prevalence of psychiatric problems in the student population; a direct comparison of helpseekers and nonhelpseekers is not made, however.

The *prospective* type tests incoming students for evidence of disturbance, identifies students who do and do not seem high in problems, and looks for differential treatment rates between the two groups. The *retrospective* type takes those students who have sought help at psychiatric facilities and compares them either to a sample of students who have not sought help at those facilities or to the general student population.

FINDINGS

Prospective studies typically reveal that students initially identified as having many or severe problems are more likely to seek help at psychiatric facilities than those identified as not having many or severe problems. Retrospective studies usually find significant differences between helpseekers and nonhelpseekers, including demographic characteristics and both relatively positive, desirable as well as negative, undesirable traits and attitudes.

The main specific findings of sixteen studies comparing helpseekers with nonhelpseekers are pooled and summarized in Tables 1–5. For convenience the variables have been grouped together in general areas. The Tables include not only significantly differentiating variables but also those which do not differentiate between the two groups, those which may but need further research before being generally accepted, those which may not but need further research, and those which have been found significant but in contrary directions in different studies.

Variables which have been found significantly related to helpseeking behavior in at least two studies, found not significant in fewer studies than the number with significant findings, *and* significantly contradicted (significant findings in the opposite direction) by none are called "probably related." Variables which have been found significant in only one study *and* significantly contradicted in none are called "possibly related." Variables which have never been found significantly related to helpseeking are called "probably unrelated." One variable which was found significant in one study but not significant in four others is also included in this category. Those which have been found significant but in different directions in different studies are designated "equivocal."

In the tables shown at the end of this chapter, phrased variables are always phrased in the way thought to be more true of helpseekers than of nonhelpseekers. The references to the studies confirming, not confirming, and contradicting the relationships are included. It should be noted that since King (1968) reported on two separate studies in a single paper, these are treated separately in counting but are referred to with the same citation.

Looking only at what apparently are the most salient variables, helpseekers, compared to nonhelpseekers, are more likely to be single and female. Their parents tend to have a higher occupational level and more frequently are separated or divorced. Academically, helpseekers tend to be in the arts, humanities, and social and behavioral sciences, and they are less often found in engineering, science, or professional schools. They have more frequently changed their course of studies and are less frequently in an area fulfilling their fathers' expectations. Overall they enjoy college less.

Social and religious group variables are clearly important. Much more frequently than nonhelpseekers, helpseekers have no religion or no preference, are Jewish, or are of some "other" religion. They are less likely to be Catholic or Protestant, and they attend church less frequently. They are less likely to be athletes and less likely to be fraternity members, and they tend to have fewer extracurricular activities. They tend to know other helpseekers.

On personality and problem variables, helpseekers have more variously defined problems than nonhelpseekers. They consult doctors more, smoke and drink more, and sleep less. They are more nervous and anxiety ridden. They tend to be restless, dissatisfied, moody, and tense. They are more self-centered. They are more apt to put their own needs before others', and they are more emotional, impulsive, aggressive, and attention getting. They are less self-confident and socially facile, and they tend less toward constructive reaction to stress. On the other hand, helpseekers are more psychologically minded than nonhelpseekers, more questioning, and more introspective. They are less authoritarian and less accepting of traditional values in and out of college. They are more cosmopolitan and more aesthetic. They are more complex in their thinking, and tend to be more autonomous.

DISCUSSION

Social and religious group variables may be key ones in understanding the differences between helpseekers and nonhelpseekers. The fraternity members, the members of athletic teams, the participants in extracurricular activities, the regular churchgoers, especially Catholic and Protestant, all are much less likely to seek help than their opposite members. Conceivably, healthier students are attracted to these groups in the first place. Possibly such affiliations tend to prevent problems from arising as frequently as for students not in such groups. It is possible that students with problems who belong to such groups tend to see appropriate recourses within the groups and seek help for problems there. And perhaps such groups have norms or beliefs less encouraging of seeking psychological help at professional counseling agencies. Helpseekers clearly tend to be members of such groups less often. Possibly their own problems, especially social difficulties, make it less likely that they will be accepted into some of these groups. Given such characteristics as being more questioning and autonomous and less authoritarian and accepting of traditional values, it would seem probable that helpseekers on the whole would choose not to become involved in these groups. More research is needed to shed more light on the specific reasons why nonhelpseekers tend to be in such groups so much more than do helpseekers.

Perhaps a more general factor that would encompass many of the variables found to differentiate helpseekers from nonhelpseekers would be the presence or absence of role models that prescribe fairly definite ways of acting and thinking. Fraternities and athletic teams may provide fairly definite role models, and religions such as the Catholic and Protestant may tend more than Jewish, "other," and "none" to prescribe definite thought and behavior. Variables other than the social and religious ones also may fit this way of looking at the differences between help-seekers and nonhelpseekers. Students in the arts, humanities, and social and behavioral sciences often tend to have much less rigid and set patterns to follow than those in engineering, science, and professional schools. Foreign students may be particularly uncertain about their roles. This uncetainty may be true to a lesser extent of graduate students, who may at once be students, spouses, parents, and employees, with some confusion over these roles. Even the tendency for helpseekers to be female might be relevant; those students might have trouble deciding between traditional, deferent, ultimately wife and mother roles, and more modern, competitive, career-oriented roles. Married students have a definite role as spouse, unlike single students. Parents of higher occupational level may have fewer specific expectations of what their children should do and become in college; it was found that helpseekers are less likely to be in a course of study fulfilling their parents' expectations. Conceivably having parents who are separated or divorced leaves students lacking role models or having conflicting expectations. Research would be needed to examine more directly whether or not the general hypothesis has any merit, but it is possible that in general helpseekers have fewer definite role models and expectations placed on them concerning how they should think and act, or at least they accept fewer than do nonhelpseekers.

Not having the support of close-knit, relatively authoritarian groups, not having the security of "knowing" how to think and what to do, and not being free of ambiguity regarding the path to be taken in college, may make personal adjustment in the college environment more difficult for the helpseeker. His sense of identity may not be easily worked out. This state of affairs could certainly contribute to anxiety, nervousness, feelings of being out of place, etc. The helpseeker's independence, lack of acceptance of the traditional and authoritarian, acceptance of ambiguity, complexity of thought, and introspection probably have their price. Taking the more difficult ways of growth and adjustment means taking on more problems as well. And for these problems the student is more likely to seek help.

Whether or not helpseeking is a sign of weakness remains debatable. Accepting that helpseekers have problems, it is a value judgment whether their other characteristics distinguishing them from nonhelpseekers represent strength or weakness. But given the goals of higher education, it is difficult not to see some of these attributes as strengths. Snyder and Kahne (1969), for instance, note that freshman users as compared to nonusers showed more of the qualities that the college values. There seems to be in the helpseeker a pattern of positive and valued qualities that may make adjustment more difficult and complex in his college years, and lead to more personal problems and adjustment difficulties, but that also may well put him ahead in the long run.

METHODOLOGICAL PROBLEMS IN STUDYING HELPSEEKER BEHAVIOR

Several problems connected with comparing helpseekers and nonhelpseekers are found in the studies reviewed here. To a certain extent some findings seem to be specific to the school or type of school studied, even significant in different directions at different schools. Since almost half the studies come from Ivy League colleges and they are of unusually high academic standing, the literature taken as a whole may be somewhat unbalanced in that direction.

A much more serious problem with most of the studies is their failure to take into account all helpseeking behavior of the students involved. Many studies compare users and nonusers of one particular agency without regard to whether students sought help for problems at other agencies. While this does not invalidate the comparison of users and nonusers of that particular agency, it leaves no assurance that a valid comparison of helpseekers and non-helpseekers in general can be made. At some colleges the facility or facilities studied may be the only formal source of counseling for students; but this may be the case less often than might be thought. Virtually all very severe disturbances that are treated at all might be treated at the sole available psychiatric facility, but most of the students facing crises can be treated in a variety of settings. For instance, as Bloom (1971) has shown, at the University of Colorado, a medium-sized university in a small city, there are no less than twenty formally organized campus agencies with counseling services for students with personal problems, a number of private professionals, groups, and public agencies in the immediate community, and a profusion of services in a nearby metropolitan area. All are used to a certain extent by students with problems. In a study done at Brooklyn College, Pearlman (1966) found that the most commonly used source of psychological counseling for students was outside private professionals, with various college facilities second, and community clinics and agencies a more distant third. Of all the studies reviewed here, only King's (1968) seems to take into consideration all possible helpseeking behavior.

Another important difficulty in interpreting most of the studies is not so much a methodological problem but rather more of a logical consideration. The findings that helpseekers as opposed to nonhelpseekers tend to have more problems and disturbances are not surprising. Many colleges have settings such that for *severely* disturbed students it is relatively hard *not* to come in contact with counseling or psychiatric agencies or personnel and still remain in school. This fact may introduce some bias into the comparison, such that in the helpseeking group are some of the moderately disturbed students and most of the severely disturbed ones, while some of the moderately disturbed ones but only a few of the severely disturbed students are in the nonhelpseeking group. Thus the differential degree of pathology among helpseekers and nonhelpseekers may account for the rate differential. There is also further reason why it is not surprising to find more evidence of disturbance among helpseekers than among nonhelpseekers. Helping facilities are, after all, primarily for students with problems. In the helpseeking group we see the student who has a problem and seeks aid in solving or coping with it; but in the nonhelpseeking group we see not only the student who has a problem and for whatever reason does not seek help for it, but also the student who isn't bothered enough by a problem to consider seeking help for it. Thus all helpseekers have the personality prerequisites for seeking help in confronting their problems; of the nonhelpseekers who do not have significant problems, some may have these traits should problems arise, but those nonhelpseekers who do have significant problems apparently do not have the traits that would lead them to seek help for the problems. If willingness or determination to seek help for problems when they arise reflects or is a product of some desirable traits, then this may partially explain why the helpseeker has a combination of desirable and undesirable traits as compared to the nonhelpseeker. The fact that the helpseeking group has a greater percentage of students with significant problems would contribute some differences in one direction, while the fact that in the helpseeking group a greater percentage of students are willing to seek help in confronting their problems might contribute to some of the desirable traits found to distinguish the helpseeker from the nonhelpseeker.

A more logical comparison than the one generally made would be to look at students who give evidence of having problems, and compare those who seek help for their problems to those who do not seek help for them. In other words, the variable of degree of problems or disturbance should be controlled when comparing helpseekers and nonhelpseekers. Only three of the studies do this. West's (1971) study produced no significant findings. Testing results reported by Scheff (1966) and Segal, Weiss, and Sokol (1965) shows that many of their finding are significant. Unfortunately none of the studies that controls for degree of problems also considers all helpseeking behavior, a major difficulty discussed earlier.

AREAS FOR FURTHER RESEARCH

There are several areas in the study of helpseeking behavior which could benefit from further research. As noted, there is a need for more studies which control for degree of problems and consider all possible helpseeking behavior. An important question is whether nonhelpseekers really do not seek help. Do they get help elsewhere, either from unexamined professional sources or, perhaps more interesting, from lay sources? Few studies have been made of why students seek or do not seek help when they have significant problems. Another important question is what differentiates students having pro-helpseeking and anti-helpseeking attitudes? Bloom's (personal communication) findings regarding freshmen in the classes of 1972 and 1974 at the University of Colorado indicate that less than fifty percent of students would be willing to seek trained help if they had a personal problem. Further research here could be applied both to those students with and without significant problem areas.

Reifler (1971) notes that further prevalence studies would not be nearly as useful as longitudinal studies which could provide incidence data in relation to other variables. Longitudinal studies including both periodic measures of students' problem levels, particularly measures geared more to the students' college adjustment and experience than are traditional measures of pathology such as the MMPI, and as broad a range as possible of factual and attitudinal data from the students, would probably be most useful. Hopefully further research will have more specific implications for developing and evaluating programs to reach students in difficulty who would otherwise be nonhelp-seekers.

REFERENCES

Baker, R. W. Incidence of psychological disturbance in college students. *Journal of the American College Health Association*, 1965, *13*, 532–540.

Bloom, B. L. Problems of ecology on the college campus: The sociocultural environment. *Journal of the American College Health Association*, 1971, *20*, 128–131.

Boyce, R. M., & Barnes, D. S. Psychiatric problems of university students. *Canadian Psychiatric Association Journal*, 1966, *11*, 49–56.

Boyce, R. M., & Thurlow, H. J. Characteristics of university students with emotional problems. *Canadian Psychiatric Association Journal*, 1969, *14*, 481–492.

Braaten, L. J., & Darling, C. D. Mental health services in college: Some statistical analyses. *Student Medicine*, 1961, *10*, 235–253.

Coons, F. W. The clinical setting of college mental health. *Journal of the American College Health Association*, 1970, *18*, 201–203.

Davie, J. S. Who uses a college mental hygiene clinic? In B. M. Wedge (Ed.), *Psychosocial problems of college men*. New Haven: Yale University Press, 1958.

King, F. W. The MMPI F scale as a predictor of lack of adaptation to college. *Journal of the American College Health Association,* 1967, *15,* 261–269.

King, S. H. Characteristics of students seeking psychiatric help during college. *Journal of the American College Health Association,* 1968, *17,* 150–156.

Kysar, J. E. Therapy with the working-class college student. *College Health,* 1967, *15,* 307–311.

Linn, L. S. Social characteristics and social interaction in the utilization of a psychiatric outpatient clinic. *Journal of Health and Social Behavior,* 1967, *8,* 3–14.

Pearlman, S. The college student views his mental health experience. *College Health,* 1966, *14,* 277–283.

Reifler, C. B. Epidemiologic aspects of college mental health. *College Health,* 1971, *19,* 159–163.

Reifler, C. B., & Liptzin, M. B. Epidemiological studies of college mental health. *Archives of General Psychiatry,* 1969, *20,* 528–540.

Reifler, C. B., Liptzin, M. B., & Fox, J. T. College psychiatry as public health psychiatry. *American Journal of Psychiatry,* 1967, *124,* 116–125.

Rust, R. M. Epidemiology of mental health in college. *The Journal of Psychology,* 1960, *49,* 235–248.

Scheff, T. J. Users and non-users of a student psychiatric clinic. *Journal of Health and Human Behavior,* 1966, *7,* 114–121.

Segal, B. E. Epidemiology of emotional disturbances among college undergraduates: A review and analysis. *Journal of Nervous and Mental Disease,* 1966, *143,* 348–362.

Segal, B. E., Walsh, T. M., & Weiss, R. J. Emotional maladjustment in an undergraduate population: An analytical assessment of six-year trends. *College Health,* 1966, *14,* 190–196.

Segal, B. E., Weiss, R. J., & Sokol, R. Emotional adjustment, social organization and psychiatric treatment rates. *American Sociological Review,* 1965, *30,* 548–556.

Snyder, B. R., & Kahne, M. J. Stress in higher education and student use of university psychiatrists. *American Journal of Orthopsychiatry,* 1969, *39,* 23–35.

Walters, O. S. Prevalence of diagnosed emotional disorders in university students. *Journal of the American College Health Association,* 1970, *18,* 204–209.

Weiss, R. J., Segal, B. E., & Sokol, R. Epidemiology of emotional disturbance in a men's college. *The Journal of Nervous and Mental Disease,* 1965, *141,* 240–249.

West, M. Sophomore students on academic probation: A comparison of users and nonusers of a university counseling facility. *College Health,* 1971, *19,* 235–238.

TABLE 1
Comparison of Helpseekers and Nonhelpseekers on Personal and Family Background Variables

	Confirmed	Not Confirmed	Contradicted
Probably Related			
Female	Boyce & Thurlow (1969) Braaten & Darling (1961) Reifler et al. (1967) Scheff (1966) Walters (1970)	Boyce & Barnes (1966)	—
Single	Boyce & Thurlow (1969) Braaten & Darling (1961) Walters (1970)	Boyce & Barnes (1966)	—
Parents separated or divorced	Boyce & Thurlow (1969) King (1968)	King (1968)	—
Parents' occupational level higher	Kysar (1967) Scheff (1966) Snyder & Kahne (1969)	Davie (1958)	—
Possibly Related			
First born, last born, or only child	—	Boyce & Barnes (1966)	—

139

TABLE 1 (cont'd)

	Confirmed	Not Confirmed	Contradicted
Probably Unrelated			
Birthplace or home state	Scheff (1966)	Boyce & Thurlow (1969) Davie (1958) King (1968)	—
Number of moves as a child	—	King (1968)	—
Parental source of authority or discipline	—	King (1969)	—
Family ethnic background	—	King (1968)	—
Family political preference	—	King (1968)	—
Parents' educational level	Scheff (1966)	Davie (1958) King (1968)	—
Family income	—	Boyce & Thurlow (1969) Davie (1958)	—

140

Father went to same college	—	Boyce & Thurlow (1969) Davie (1958) King (1969)
Financial status	—	Davie (1958)
Family size	—	Davie (1958)
Age at parents' separation	—	Boyce & Thurlow (1969)
Equivocal		
Younger	Boyce & Thurlow (1969)	Boyce & Barnes (1966) Reifler *et al.* (1967)

141

TABLE 2

Comparison of Helpseekers and Nonhelpseekers on Academic Variables

Probably Related	Confirmed	Not Confirmed	Contradicted
In arts, humanities, or social and behavioral sciences	Boyce & Barnes (1966) Braaten & Darling (1961) Scheff (1966)	Boyce & Thurlow (1969)	—
Not in engineering, science, professional schools	Boyce & Barnes (1966) Braaten & Darling (1961) Scheff (1966) Walters (1970)	Boyce & Thurlow (1969)	—
Have changed course of studies	Boyce & Barnes (1966) Boyce & Thurlow (1969)	—	—
Not in course fulfilling father's expectations	Boyce & Barnes (1966) Boyce & Thurlow (1969)	—	—
Less satisfied with freshman year	King (1968)	—	—
Did not have a good time at college	Davie (1958) King (1968)	King (1968)	—
Foreign student	Braaten & Darling (1961) Walters (1970)	—	—

142

Possibly Related

Graduate student	Walters (1970)	Boyce & Barnes (1966)	—
More dissatisfied with secondary school	King (1968)	King (1968)	—
Went to secondary school in larger city	Scheff (1966)	—	—
More critical of college	Davie (1958)	—	—
Favorite features of college not social, interpersonal, or extracurricular	Davie (1958)	—	—
Would have preferred different college	Davie (1958)	—	—
Considered leaving for another college	Davie (1968)	—	—
Less study per week	Boyce & Thurlow (1969)	—	—
Lower final grades	Boyce & Thurlow (1969)	Davie (1958)	—
In academic trouble	Braaten & Darling (1961)	Davie (1958)	—
Attended one or more universities prior to present one	Boyce & Barnes (1966)	Boyce & Thurlow (1969)	—

143

TABLE 2 (cont'd)

Probably Unrelated	Confirmed	Not Confirmed	Contradicted
Type of secondary school	—	Davie (1958) King (1968)	—
Secondary school rank	—	King (1968)	—
Participation or offices held in high school organization	—	King (1968)	—
SAT scores, predicted college rank	—	King (1968)	—
Certainty about right choice of college	—	King (1968)	—
Predicted GPA	—	Davie (1958)	—
Year enjoyed, development most and least	—	Davie (1958)	—
Suggested changes in college education	—	Davie (1958)	—
Future plans	—	Davie (1958)	—
Equivocal			
Freshman or lower year in college	Braaten & Darling (1961)	Boyce & Thurlow (1969)	Reifler *et al.* (1967)

144

TABLE 3

Comparison of Helpseekers and Nonhelpseekers on Social and
Religious Group Variables

	Confirmed	Not Confirmed	Contradicted
Probably Related			
Not in a fraternity	Boyce & Barnes (1966) Braaten & Darling (1961) Segal *et al.* (1965)	Davie (1958)	—
Less in sports or athletics	Boyce & Thurlow (1969) Davie (1958) Segal *et al.* (1965)	—	—
Know other helpseekers	Boyce & Barnes (1966) Linn (1967)	—	—
Religion none or no preference	Boyce & Barnes (1966) Boyce & Thurlow (1969) Braaten & Darling (1961) Davie (1958) King (1968) Scheff (1966) Walters (1970)	—	—
Religion "other"	Boyce & Barnes (1966) King (1968)	—	—

145

TABLE 3 (cont'd)

	Confirmed	Not Confirmed	Contradicted
Religion Jewish	Braaten & Darling (1961) Scheff (1966) Segal et al. (1965)	—	—
Not Catholic or Protestant	Braaten & Darling (1961) King (1968) Scheff (1966) Segal et al. (1965)	—	—
Less frequent attendance at any church	King (1968) Scheff (1966)	—	—
Possibly Related			
Attendance at a specific church	King (1968)	King (1968)	—
Political preference none or independent	King (1968)	King (1968)	—
Greater percentage of friends seen as having social or emotional problems	Linn (1967)	—	—
More often engaged in discussion of social and emotional problems with friends	Linn (1967)	—	—

146

Fewer close friends	Scheff (1966)	—	—
Lower frequency of dating last year	Scheff (1966)	—	—
Fewer or no extracurricular activities	Boyce & Barnes (1966) Boyce & Thurlow (1969) Scheff (1966)	Davie (1958) King (1968)	—
Probably Unrelated			
Friends entering same college	—	King (1968)	—
Family religion	—	King (1968)	—
Study alone or with company	—	King (1968)	—
Time spent on extracurricular activities	—	King (1968)	—
Equivocal			
Noncollege housing	Boyce & Barnes (1966) Reifler et al. (1967)	—	Braaten & Darling (1961)

147

TABLE 4

Comparison of Helpseekers and Nonhelpseekers on Health-Related Variables

Probably Related	Confirmed	Not Confirmed	Contradicted
Smoke more	Boyce & Barnes (1966) Boyce & Thurlow (1969)	—	—
Drink more	Boyce & Barnes (1966) Boyce & Thurlow (1969)	—	—
Sleep less	Boyce & Barnes (1966) Boyce & Thurlow (1969)	—	—
Consulted doctors more	Boyce & Thurlow (1969) Davie (1958) King (1968) Snyder & Kahne (1969)	—	—
Significant recent weight change	Boyce & Barnes (1966) Boyce & Thurlow (1969)	—	—

Possibly Related

Drink not at all	Boyce & Thurlow (1969)	—	—
Fewer colds, less hair loss	Boyce & Thurlow (1969)	—	—
More insomnia, migraine, chronic skin disorder	Boyce & Thurlow (1969)	—	—
Lower evaluation of past health	King (1968)	King (1968)	—

Probably Unrelated

Number of recent illnesses, different illnesses, time off school due to illness, accidents, dental work, number of hospitalizations	—	Boyce & Thurlow (1969)	—
Cronic illnesses, born handicaps, congenital disorders	—	Boyce & Thurlow (1969)	—
Hay fever, dysmenorrhea, asthma, allergies	—	Boyce & Thurlow (1969)	—

TABLE 5
Comparison of Helpseekers and Nonhelpseekers on Personality and Problem Variables

	Confirmed	Not Confirmed	Contradicted
Probably Related			
More nervous	Boyce & Thurlow (1969) Davie (1958)	—	—
More anxious	Davie (1958) King (1968) Snyder & Kahne (1969)	King (1968)	—
Lower social desirability	King (1968)	—	—
Lower need deference	King (1968)	—	—
Higher need emotionality	King (1968)	—	—
Lower sensation	King (1968)	—	—
Higher impulse expression	King (1968)	—	—
Higher unconscious strain	King (1968)	—	—
Lower constructive reaction	King (1968)	—	—
Frequently felt out of place at college	Davie (1958) King (1968)	King (1968)	—

Worse on MMPI	King (1967) Segal et al. (1966) Segal et al. (1965) Weiss et al. (1965)	—	—
Lower F scale	King (1968)	—	—
More psychologically minded	King (1968)	—	—
Higher intuition	King (1968)	—	—
Higher introspection	Linn (1967)	—	—
	Snyder & Kahne (1969)		
Possibly Related			
More loneliness	Davie (1958)	—	—
More problems (Rust scale)	Rust (1960)	—	—
Higher need to be aggressive	King (1968)	King (1968)	
Higher need for self-display and attention seeking	King (1968)	King (1968)	
Lower effectiveness in dealing with others	King (1968)	King (1968)	
Lower self-confidence	King (1968)	King (1968)	

TABLE 5 (cont'd)

	Confirmed	Not Confirmed	Contradicted
Lower self-acceptance	King (1968)	King (1968)	—
Higher schizoid functioning	Snyder & Kahne (1969)	—	—
More moody, procrastinating, restless, dissatisfied, high strung, rebellious, tense	Davie (1958)	—	—
Less relaxed, calm, efficient, prompt, self-controlled, consistent	Davie (1958)	—	—
Lower traditional value orientation	King (1968)	King (1968)	—
Higher cosmopolitan identification	Linn (1967)	—	—
Lower college identification	Linn (1967)	—	—
Higher aestheticism	Snyder & Kahne (1969)	—	—
Higher religious liberalism	Snyder & Kahne (1969)	—	—
Higher complexity	Snyder & Kahne (1969)	—	—
Higher autonomy	Snyder & Kahne (1969)	—	—
More sensitive, idealistic	Davie (1958)	—	—

152

7. Aspects of Campus Mental Health Outside of the United States and Canada

SAMUEL PEARLMAN

As the author has indicated in a previous publication (Pearlman, 1968), the arraignment of mental illness as the "most insidious of human afflictions [Srole, *et al.*, 1962, p. 8]" has had its counterpart in higher education in the recognition of the high personal losses in efficiency, social relationships, and career mobility among college students as the outcome of affective dysfunction. In international terms, the United States has been comparatively in the forefront of both research and action in developing an awareness of this campus mental health situation, and in instituting programs with both preventive and treatment orientations. The beginnings of this movement go back to the period following the first World War, reached a moderate peak of expansion during the late thirties, at about the time that Fry and Rostow were writing their stimulating volume on *Mental Health in College* (1942), slowed in pace during the subsequent war years, and then resurged through the next few decades. The rising interest and concern were paralleled by a "publication explosion," which by conservative estimate resulted in a tripling of the amount of literature in this field within a single generation (Yale, undated; Funkenstein & Wilkie, 1956; Pearlman, 1966). It was only a matter of course, during the latter part of this modern era, for surveys of ongoing campus mental health programs and their related epidemiologies to appear in significant numbers (American Psychiatric Association, 1954; Ginsburg, 1955; Gundle & Kraft, 1956; Group for the Advancement of Psychiatry, 1957, 1962; Cass, 1961; Robbins, 1963; Congdon & Lothrop, 1963; Nugent & Pareis, 1965; Pearlman, 1968; Bloom, 1970a, 1970b), and for a number of books to be issued with a focus on this subject (Farnsworth, 1957; Wedge, 1958; Whittington, 1963; Blaine & McArthur, 1971).

The international picture outside of the United States and Canada did not have as rapid or detailed a development, for understandable reasons. Recovery of the older universities from the impact of the Second World War proved to be slow; in both old and new countries, moreover, as an outcome of the gradual removal of elitist qualification for admission, student populations burgeoned with such force as to require the expansion of old and new institutions of higher learning. Traditional frameworks of education came under great pressure, and in these evolving circumstances, campus mental health as an area of concern did not receive a high priority for action.

Viewed broadly, the international progression into programming for campus mental health tended to move through three identifiable phases, not necessarily sequential nor with similar emphases in various countries. Admittedly, the nature and quality of this progression were functions of a nation's sociocultural history, its demographic expansion, the level of its urbanization and industrialization, and its political set. Additionally important at times was the willingness of a nation to accept another (or another region) as a model for its own university development, or to use professional consultative resources of other lands in support of its own campus mental health designs. Of these phases, the first was typically focused on raising the level of awareness of student health needs generally and of their related mental health aspects. The second development was characterized by an emphasis on epidemiology, that is, on the research into student life, student characteristics, and student health, as these related to the university environment. The third phase involved the application of such understanding and knowledge as were forthcoming from the first two phases to the actual programming of mental health efforts.

RAISING THE LEVEL OF AWARENESS

Over the years the rise of national interest in the emotional problems of university students has been coincident (among other factors) with an expansion of the training of professional individuals, a few of whom tended to be attached either to university health or counseling services, often in an unplanned fashion. About a decade and a half ago, in the United States and Canada, there were fewer than 100 colleges and universities (out of a total of 728 two- and four-year institutions) which were found to be maintaining special facilities to deal with students' emotional problems; and of these institutions, 87 had psychiatrists, 52 had psychologists, and 17 had social workers, either on full-time or part-time assignments (Gundle & Kraft, 1956). Except for the larger institutions, which tended to have well-developed mental health services, the focus of attention was on emergent situations of relatively few students. The numbers of mental health professionals have increased materially to date, and one has but to examine the roster of membership of the Mental Health Section of the American College Health Association to attest to this fact. Nevertheless, in the light of demographic projection by 1975 of nearly 9 million young people enrolled in institutions of higher learning in the United States, the present status and efforts of the university mental health services cannot be considered adequate (Pearlman, 1968). This situation has been typical of the nations that are considered advanced and, more often than not, will be found to characterize the western European universities.

In the less advanced or newer countries, this trend has hardly been as manifest. University populations have significantly expanded here as well, and increasing attention has been accorded to the general health circumstances of students. Nevertheless, in terms of the mental health needs of students, there has been a considerable lag in development. To the limited extent that mental health services do exist, credit should be assigned to the concerns and devotion of a few professionals in these countries (mostly psychiatrists like G. A. German in Uganda, L. S. Melki in Lebanon, E.-k. Yeh in Taiwan, K. Savonen and Y. O. Alanen in Finland, M. A. Fazal in Kenya, F. W. Wright-Short in Australia, and T. A. Lambo in Nigeria, among others) who have either been exposed to specialized training in lands other than their own, or have been in constructive contact with other individuals through international associations and conferences.

The import of these international associations and conferences, which in whole or in part dealt with student health matters, cannot be minimized. Their prime utility has been in shaping the contexts within which information and experience could be shared among the participants and then channeled back to their respective universities and countries. While these groups in the main have been of a voluntary (nongovernmental) character, they were often able to solicit formal or informal government sponsorship. Several of these, among others, warrant note: the World Union of Organizations for the Safeguard of Youth, the Interamerican Society of Psychology, the International Association of Social Psychiatry. Coordinate with their partial efforts in the area of campus mental health has been the trend toward the inclusion of interested foreign registrants in the regular conferences of national associations and in the commemorative meetings of special institutions, *viz.*, the 50th anniversary meeting of the American College Health Association, Boston, April, 1970 (Pearlman, 1970), and the Symposium on Psychological Disorders among Students in celebration of the 20th anniversary of the founding of the Free University of Berlin, Berlin, March, 1968 (Ziolko, 1968). These annual, special, or regional meetings have been held at various points in the world, so that they have been a natural stimulus to the growth of interest in student mental health in the countries in which the deliberations have taken place. Many of their meetings have an inbuilt factor of periodicity and have therefore been able to maintain the currency of their impact on the developing student mental health movement. Their published reports and proceedings have supplemented this influence long after the close of the conference sessions.

The International Student Service (now known as World University Service, with headquarters at Geneva) is one of the very few in existence which was able to hold international or regional meetings prior to the outbreak of World War II—in 1933 at Leysin, Switzerland, and in 1939 at Zurich. It has since organized "experts' conferences" on student health in Denmark (1949), Singapore (1951), Switzerland (1961), Ceylon (1962), and Thailand (1966). The flavor of these conferences (whose proceedings are noted in the references) is well illustrated by the one held in Switzerland (1961): the participants came from twelve European countries, and were joined by observers from Burma, Ceylon, India, and the Philippines, along with representatives from the World Health Organization, the Office of the United Nations High Commissioner for Refugees, the International Federation of Medical Students' Associations, and the International Association of Universities. The following is a sampling of the papers and reports on student mental health presented to the workshops of this Swiss Conference:

Care of mental health of students at higher schools and universities in Poland. S. Cwybar, Poland.

The incidence, variety, and severity of symptoms of
psychological ill-health occurring among univer-
sity students. R. J. Still, United Kingdom.
Student mental health problems in Yugoslavia. V. O.
Savic, Yugoslavia.
Student mental health and facilities for treatment:
the University of Oslo, Norway. A. Haagenrud,
Norway.
Student mental health program at the Philippine
Women's University. E. Aldaba-Lim, the Philip-
pines.
Reflections on the advancement of student mental
hygiene in Switzerland. G. Bally, Switzerland.

Both the World Federation for Mental Health (WFMH)
and the World Health Organization (WHO) have sponsored conference activity on international and regional
levels, parts of which have from time to time touched on
student mental health. By way of example, mention can
be made of the central theme of the 19th annual WFMH
conference (Prague, 1966), "Public Health, Education
and Mental Hygiene," which encompassed several technical sessions on university mental health services; about
25 countries had representation, mostly from Europe, in
this instance. The regional WFMH assemblies have only
irregularly given attention to the subject of university
mental health, and one of the better illustrations of this
type of workshop was that held in Cairo (1970), involving
some 300 participants from five Arab and three European
countries (WFMH *Bulletin,* 1970/71). Probably the most
important earlier WFMH-sponsored meeting on this
topic was the first International Conference on Student
Mental Health, held in September, 1956, in Princeton,
New Jersey, which interestingly enough, came up with a
definition of student *mental health* which contained
nothing directly connotative of *mental illness:* "The men-
tally healthy person is one who is developing toward personal maturity. Maturity is reached in the same degree as
the individual can independently and in a fruitful way

overcome his internal conflicts, realize his own aims in life and responsibly live in fellowship with others [Funkenstein, 1959, pp. 417–418.]" In balance, the delegates at this Conference did emphasize that positive mental health did not mean adjustment under all circumstances, conformity, freedom from anxiety and tension, constant happiness, the absence of personal idiosyncrasies, the undermining of authority, or an opposition to religious values.

The pattern of activity of the World Health Organization, one of the specialized intergovernmental agencies of the United Nations, has been similar to that of the WFMH. Several of its meetings, both international and regional, have been concerned with mental health conditions generally and with university health services in particular, and a few of its widely disseminated publications have centered on these same themes. One of its major "expert committees," for example, undertook an assessment in 1965 of the status and function of university health services, and issued the following motivational pronouncement on campus mental health:

> Problems of mental health are regarded as among the most important and time-consuming with which the UHS [University Health Service] has to deal . . . not so much because of the proportion of students seeking help but because trivial difficulties can sometimes cause serious impairment of intellectual efficiency, even in the most able students. On the other hand, a serious mental breakdown is not necessarily followed by a mediocre career. Skilled management and treatment ranging from simple support during a temporary crisis to more sophisticated forms of psychiatric care can frequently aid in the resolution of these difficulties. A full range of care should therefore be provided through the UHS. . . . From a preventive point of view, it is a function of the UHS to be alert to those academic, administrative and disciplinary elements in the university unfavourable to

the sound development of the personality and likely
to provoke unnecessary psychological stress [WHO
Technical Report Series, No. 320, 1966, pp. 13–15].

This world-wide imprimatur on these guidelines for
university mental health was followed a year later (1966)
by a regional European Symposium on Student Health
Services, which met in Cracow, Poland, and was attended
by 19 participants and observers nominated by the governments of European countries. The report of this conference, while admitting that international discussion of
university health services "has not been frequent," went
on to state that "through international contracts he [the
practitioner] may learn of new solutions that can be applied to his local problems, and he may gain courage from
the fact that colleagues in other places face the same
difficulties as he does [WHO Regional Office for Europe,
1967, p. 1]."

All these organizations, by their very existence as well
as their activities of the past two decades, have had considerable world influence in highlighting the campus
mental health situation, in pointing up the reflected
needs, and in determining the directions to be taken in
structure and service. Admittedly, no single model for a
university mental service evolved out of the international
deliberations, since recognition was continually given to
the unique character of the higher-education development of each nation or region. The conferences, however,
have served as a positive stimulus to research in campus
mental health, and while the *who, what, how,* and *where*
of the epidemiological picture have as yet an understandable vagueness, limning data are currently more available
than ever before. As indicated earlier, the search for well-
grounded information on campus mental health has con-
stituted a second-phase endeavor in response to patently
needed developments [*cf.* p. 155, *supra.*].

THE INTERNATIONAL EPIDEMIOLOGICAL SCENE

There is no single source of data, descriptive or statistical, on college or university mental health in an international sense. Published reports and articles are to be found scattered through a variety of national and international journals, in most instances written in their respective national languages, and are therefore not always available for ready collation and comparison. The need for a single international depository is manifest, and it would logically fall to an international association like the World Federation for Mental Health or the World University Service to undertake a project along this line.

It is but natural that most of the published reports at hand are derived from the countries which are considered to be well developed, and for the most part these are (apart from the United States and Canada) focused on Western Europe. In *England,* using a questionnaire to assess the incidence of psychological handicap among third-year Cambridge undergraduates, Davy (1957) found that 15.5% of his sample felt depressed, apathetic, apprehensive, and under strain; a quarter of these men had already sought expert advice about their psychological problems, and a further quarter stated that they would have liked to have done so. A somewhat similar outcome was derived by R. J. Still (1959) from his ten-year survey of the mental health of Leeds University students: of the 10,500 men and women seen by the University Health Service, 14.7% presented psychological symptoms of some degree of severity. In reviewing one year's intake of matriculants at University College, London, Malleson (1958) reported that 20% of them had handicapping psychiatric disorders of varying severity; serious disorders were found to reach the level of 4%, a figure which was only moderately higher than that of Davy (1960) at Cambridge. A later canvass and followup by Kidd (1965) of 1,555 first-year students at the University of Edinburgh revealed a prevalence rate for psychiatric disorders of 9% for men and 14.6% for women, markedly similar to the data collected by him and his colleague (Kidd & Caldbeck-Meenan, 1966) at the Queen's University of Belfast. Reports of investigations of this type, with variable outcomes for different student groups, have appeared in the professional literature published in the United Kingdom: from the middle-fifties to date, no fewer than 140 items were annotated in the bibliography on student mental health of Lucas and Linken (1970).

In *France,* where the university population expanded from roughly 100,000 immediately after World War II to 600,000 by 1968, the restructuring of the university system was accompanied by a remarkable surge of interest in student mental health. The numerous obstacles in the way of a constructive response to this interest have been well described by Douady (1970), but it has been quite evident, considering the tremendous absorption of professional resources in action programs, that relatively few epidemiological reports have been issued. When it came to the preparation of a general plan for the advancement of mental health in the university environment, the National University Committee on Mental Health resorted in 1958 to the patterned "rule of three" as set forth previously by the World Health Organization: out of every 1,000 students, one must expect

—300 who, at some time during their academic careers, would encounter psychological difficulties requiring counseling;
—30 who would need to resort to specialized diagnostic centers where, eventually, they would be afforded ambulatory treatment; and
—3 who would need to undergo hospitalization for patent mental illness.

There is no comprehensive bibliography in *Spain* dealing specifically with student mental health and written by mental health specialists. More than half of the university students in the country are concentrated in Madrid and Barcelona, and about nine out of every ten students live outside of the residence-hall arrangements of the various campuses. Such data as have been derived from the students in the residence halls ("colegios mayores") are clearly unreliable (Claramunt, 1969, 1970), but mention has been made of such pathological expressions as withdrawal (in some instances to be diagnosed as schizophrenia), anxiety states, hypochondriacal reactions, and, particularly, ulcers.

In *Italy*, the University of Rome, as the largest of the Italian universities, had a registration in 1968 of about 70,000 students, of whom 27% were not expected to complete their degree courses in the designated time. During the prior 3-½ years, psychiatric examinations were accomplished on over 6,000 of its students from the major university faculties, most of whom were self-referred or were referrals from the Center of Preventive Medicine. One out of every five of these students was included as part of a (somewhat unbalanced) control group. Within the total cohort, the diagnosis of psychosis was assigned to 2.5%; twenty percent were considered to fall within the normal range, while the balance of the students manifested, by and large, various psychoneurotic and character disorders. Within the control group, an assessment of normality was accorded to more than half (57%) of the students, but the same scattering of psychiatric diagnoses was noted here as with the referred contingent, although to a much lesser degree (Frighi, 1970). In the total of examined students, the moderate psychic disturbances were the most numerous, but among the males the percentage of severe mental disorders was greater than among the females. At the university of Bologna and the University of Salerno, on a smaller five-year base of referred students (1957–1962), the percentage of psychoses reached 6.2, of psychoneuroses 23.4, of psychosomatic disorders 4.8, and of acute environmental reactions 62.8

(Frighi, 1970). Several other similar reports—generally based on already-known-to-be disturbed students—are available from several other Italian universities, but the obvious present need in Italy is for epidemiological surveys of the generality of student bodies. Perhaps the current study in progress at the University of Palermo of 5,000 young people will produce data of a broader mental health character.

In his summary of the situation in *West Germany,* Ziolko (1970) found the frequency of disorders and complaints among students to be "conspicuous." A Heidelberg survey of 2% of the student population revealed that 52% were "encumbered in their working ability," most heavily in about one-third of the investigated cases. An extrapolation of the data from various institutions in West Berlin pointed up the distinct possibility that from 10 to 20% of the student bodies were in need of mental health services.

In the *Netherlands,* with a population of nearly 13,000,000 in 1969, student attendance in higher education reached a total of 85,000, and this figure is expected to rise by more than 50% during the coming decade. Arrangements for university mental health service (Vali-Wohl & Hut, 1970) have been evolving slowly, and in general, touch only limited numbers of students (1 to 3% of the student bodies), but there is clear recognition at present among professional workers as well as by the national administration of the "hogescholen" (institutions of higher education) that these low percentages are analogous to the revealed tip of an iceberg. In the instance of the better developed health service of the University at Groningen, 1,679 individuals applied for mental health assistance (3.7% of the student body in 1967), and in 20% of these cases were accorded the numerical diagnosis of "5" (psychoses, neuroses, and other anomalies of the personality structure). As in other countries, the students with emotional problems were not required to seek help at the university, so that the number of them making off-campus, private contacts was not usually known.

In *Belgium,* one study indicated that the proportion of failures among first-year students within its four major universities reached the level of about 50%. About one out of every five students who sought assistance at the University of Louvain was labeled as having a personality disturbance, with an implication that some part of the manifest reactivity was precipitated out of exposure to examination pressures. At the University's Center for Psychotherapy, in the very recent period, there were 1,500 consultations with distressed students, of whom 100 remained in continued treatment (van de Voorde, 1970). The situation at the Free University of Brussels has been described as no less drastic (Bloch, 1970; Bloch & Rapoport-Schoonbroodt, 1970).

The Scandinavian picture of university health services is heavily bound up with social welfare systems and national insurance programs (MacHaffie & Nelson, 1969). In *Sweden,* at the University of Uppsala, the resources of the institution were swamped with calls for evaluation and treatment of psychiatric and general medical problems, on the basis of the insistence of the state directors of the National Health Service on adequate psychiatric coverage of students even at the expense of general medical care. The major psychiatric problems noted here were those of adjustment and alcoholism. At the University of Oslo, *Norway,* the psychiatrist and psychologist had been seeing about 240 students annually, and in this instance as well alcoholism was considered by the health service as its worst drug problem. In *Finland,* it was reported that 1.2% of the students in Helsinki (in 1965) consulted psychiatrists of the Student Health Service. Psychiatric examinations during this year of a sample of 269 beginning university students revealed signs of mental disturbance —mostly neurotic, of a comparatively mild degree— within 23% of them (Alanen, *et al.,* 1968). A more thorough follow-up investigation of these same individuals during their third and fourth years of study revealed an increase in the incidence of psychic disturbances (to 29%): "a real deterioration of mental health quite clearly had happened among many subjects which seems to indicate that certain environmental factors during studies are able to impair the psychic balance [Vauhkonen, *et al.*, 1969, p. 14]." For five out of the seven university centers in Finland during 1968, with registered students numbering slightly over 50,000, Holmström (1970) stated that between 1 and 2% consulted the psychiatrists of the Student Health Foundation services, and that of this percentage, over four-fifths were classified as having neuroses or neurotic symptoms.

Within the sphere of eastern Europe, only moderate attention has been given to university mental health problems. In *Czechoslovakia*, reports on the medical students at Purkyně University (Brno) and Charles University (Prague) indicated a "neuroticism" prevalence of more than 6%, more so among the women than the men (Bouchal & Jaroš, 1970; Bouchal, *et al.*, 1967). A recent study in *Poland* of several hundred second-year university students observed that "essential mental disturbances" did not exceed 5%, but did admit that 18% of these same individuals had been treated in earlier years for neurotic symptomatology (Gerard, *et al.*, 1970). In the course of the past five years, in *Romania*, evidence derived from the medical management of university students pointed to a rate of 1.35% for the schizophrenic patterns, 2.07% for the manic-depressive psychoses, and 1.14% for the psychopathies (Pirozynski, *et al.*, 1970). *Greece* has ten state universities and graduate schools, in addition to fifteen two-year teacher training colleges and several other specialized institutions; about 50,000 students are involved within this framework. The limited available data on student mental health are based on the referrals to the outpatient clinics of the university hospitals. At Athens University, 114 students were dealt with during the first nine months of its clinic's existence, and according to a rough diagnostic classification, 72 were labeled as neurotics, 30 as psychotics, 9 as borderline cases, and three as neurological cases. A more detailed study of nearly 100 students showed a somewhat similar diagnostic distribution. At the Aristotelian University at Salonica, of 75 cases randomly selected from the cohort of referred individuals, 26 students presented anxiety states, 27 psychosomatic conditions without overt anxiety, 9 psychasthenic reactions, and 3 reactive depressions; 3 schizophrenic psychotics were also identified (Gedeon, 1970).

In Africa, the only significant reports have stemmed from Makerere University College in Kampala, *Uganda*, the oldest institution of higher education in East Africa (German & Arya, 1969; German, 1970). The institution's registration tripled during the past decade and a half, and of the 1,351 undergraduates in 1967, nearly 85% consulted with the College Medical Officer. Of these using students, one out of every nine was rated as having a psychiatric problem, in most instances falling within one or another of the neurotic classifications. Psychoses were stated as relevant to nearly 7% of the attending students, and the remainder were designated as having personality disorders. The patterns represented here showed striking similarities with those of some British universities which employed somewhat the same diagnostic criteria.

The same dearth of research is apparent in the Asian continent; whatever has been of significance in the epidemiological output on the subject of university mental health has been published within the past five years. Mention should particularly be made of the continuing project, launched in 1967, of the East-West Center of the University of Hawaii, under the title of "Culture and Mental Health in Asia and the Pacific." Its endeavors have served to bring together numbers of individuals for shared discussions and reports, in many instances on school and university mental health, and its *Newsletter* has recently begun to have a wide international circulation.

In a study of medical-school dropouts in *Japan* over a period of eleven years (Shimazaki, *et al.*, 1966), the conclusion was clearly made that "one of the most urgent problems facing the student health service of our university is how to prevent the dropping out due to mental disorders [p. 311]." The incidence rate of these school-leavers was 10.4% of the total number of dropouts, and this percentage was essentially divided in two equal categories by the diagnosis of schizophrenia and the personality disorders. It was noteworthy, however, that about half of these dropouts were able in due time to complete their courses of professional study, following treatment and convalescence. At the National Tokyo University, as an outcome of the two-step interview approach applied to newly enrolled students by the psychiatric staff of the University Health Center, about 12 to 15% of the freshmen were considered to warrant mental health attention; indeed, more than three-quarters of all the schizophrenics in the university were screened out by this method (Ishicawa, 1967).

The prospective studies by Yeh and his colleagues (1967, 1970) in *Taiwan* were admirable in design and thoroughness. The investigators' examinations of a total freshman population at the National Normal University revealed the prevalence rate of psychosis to be 0.17%. A random sample ($N = 313$) of these freshmen brought out the following: 5.1% showed a symptom pattern which could be regarded as "definitely psychiatric," 25.6% were described as "highly probably psychiatric," 39.6% were not regarded as "psychiatric cases" but were exhibiting some symptoms suggesting closer observation, while only 29.7% were rated as free of any kind of symptom. More detailed psychiatric examinations were given to the same students ($N = 264$) at the end of their senior year, and no significant changes in pattern were manifest from their earlier freshman profiles. There were some data proffered by Wright-Short (1967) for *Australia:* he is one of two part-time psychiatric consultants at the University of Sydney, which has a student population of 16,000, and on the basis of his experience he projected a probability that 640 students would require skilled psychiatric help and that

160 were due to suffer serious mental breakdown during their academic careers. In *New Zealand,* Ironside (1966) assessed the psychiatric status of nearly all of the fifth-year medical students, all of whom had already gone through at least four years of a rigorous curriculum. Using the MMPI as his basic screening instrument, and following up the test outcomes with interviews of well over half the students, he found that 13.4% of the students were psychiatrically ill with clearly recognizable clinical syndromes to which orthodox diagnostic labels could be attached—"they suffered from neuroses, psychophysiological and character disorders, and five students were frankly psychotic [p. 52]."

The above materials have been presented superficially, with no pretense to completeness of survey. The available epidemiological data were considerably more detailed, but have had to be dealt with here in a most sketchy form. Moreover, within the narrow limits of this presentation, only a few countries and regions are represented. Nevertheless, the flavor of the international scene in an epidemiological framework can easily be derived. Mental health problems among university students are in evidence to some degree in every high educational institution of the world, and are being accorded increasing concern as the deprivation to each nation of the leadership potentials of disturbed students becomes more patent. It must be borne in mind that most of the reported research in this area is as yet derived from the efforts of a few individuals, and that coordinate endeavors to gather needed information, on either a regional or international level, still have a long way to go in development.

INTERNATIONAL ASPECTS OF UNIVERSITY MENTAL HEALTH PROGRAMS

In 1954, the World University Service (WUS, 1955), in cosponsorship with the International Federation of Medical Student Associations, undertook a world-wide canvass of university mental health services, and included in its queries a solicitation of information on the provision of mental hygiene assistance to students. Institutions of forty nations responded with varying degrees of data completeness. Within half of the reporting countries, such provision proved to be a nullity, and in the other half it was noted (without reference to extent) that advisory consultation with a psychiatrist or clinical psychologist was available in all or some centers of higher learning. Formal structures for the rendering of services were few and far between, but were somewhat more typical of the advanced nations. This total pattern was relevant to the times. During the following decade and a half, as a result of the several stimuli described above, certain advances in the desired direction were achieved. The movement was slow in pace and usually followed a specific sequence:

—as university health services in general settled themselves in stable fashion into university structures, consultative mental health resources of the non-university community were called upon in time of need;

—where an institution was large enough to have a medical school, an arrangement was made to use some amount of the time of the staff of its psychiatric or neurological department;

—at the point when student mental health emergencies rose in such numbers as to require a revision of the meaning of the term "emergency," part-time psychiatric assignments were made to the health service; toward the latter part of this phase, a trend occurred in the employment of psychologists and (at times) social workers;

—toward the end of this development, when research lent substance to need, there was the establishment of a formal mental health center, staffed limitedly with full- and part-time workers.

By 1964, in the United Kingdom (Wright-Short, 1967), out of 31 universities surveyed, there were 12 which employed a part-time psychiatrist and 2 which included a psychologist in their health-service frameworks. Facilities for both in-patient and out-patient treatment within a single institution were relatively rare. At Oxford, in the main, psychiatric service was still (1966) provided for the students through the National Health Service by a local psychiatrist or the local hospital in the town—a situation which brought forth demands by at least two university groups for the establishment of a comprehensive health service (Lancet, 1967). In France, centers of preventive medicine were established for all universities by a national decree of 1946, but these were largely focused on tuberculosis and other physical illnesses and did not direct their attention until very recently to mental health problems. For the most part, the task of screening and referring disturbed students in the French universities fell to the female social workers attached to the institutions. For the handling of referred students, there are presently ten universities which have Offices for University Psychological Assistance, each of which is staffed by social workers, psychologists, and specially trained teachers, backed up by psychiatrists in time of need. The pride and joy of the French system, so to speak, is based on the operation of the several medico-psychological centers of the Foundation for the Health of French Students (Douady, 1970). In actuality, these centers are small mental hospitals affiliated with the respective universities, and are exclusively available to students who cannot be treated in an ambulatory status but are yet able, during the period of hospitalization, to maintain themselves in their studies. This writer had the opportunity in 1971 to visit one of these centers (at Sceaux), and was impressed with the skilled integration of psychiatric in-patient treatment with parallel education rehabilitation.

The Mental Hygiene Service of the University of Rome, established in 1965, currently has a staff of six part-time psychiatrists and one social worker, dealing with an average of 150 new cases per month, about a quarter of whom return to the Service for additional help or other reasons. The scope of the mental health needs press for further solution, and according to the Service's director, "there is an urgency to expand (possibly by tripling) our psychiatric staff and the professional hours at its disposal, to institute a system of day hospitalization, and to establish therapeutic study groups [Frighi, 1970]." No nationally regulated and uniform framework exists for the mental health care of students in the Netherlands, so that the patterns of service vary somewhat from one institution to another. Psychiatric help is generally provided for by the polyclinics of the university hospital as well as by the local hospitals, generally without charge to the students. Three of the larger university towns have institutes for medical psychotherapy, which serve their respective communities as well as the students who live in the area. In general, the cost of mental health care for students is partially subsidized by the Foundation for Student Health Care, but extended psychotherapeutic help can only be managed through special arrangements. The 1969 data on staff support show only a moderate increase in professional workers in the university settings: for each 10,000 students there are now 2.6 psychologists, 0.7 psychiatrists, 3.2 physicians, and 4.0 deans (Vali-Wohl & Hut, 1970). No student mental health program is structured at present in Denmark (MacHaffie & Nelson, 1969), but the Danish National Health Plan incorporates a coinsurance system providing for some mental health assistance to the citizenry, including students. At the University of Copenhagen, however, there is an experimental clinic set up to deal with the students' emotional problems. In the other Scandinavian countries, university mental health provisions are somewhat more ordered: at Uppsala, Sweden, there are two full-time psychiatrists in the health service, and at Oslo, Norway, there is one part-time psychiatrist and one part-time psychologist within a similar service setting. Here, too, the government and a national health insurance plan are involved in financial support.

These are but a few illustrations of the ongoing situation; elsewhere, outside of Europe, the provisions for university mental health care are even more meager. It is to be remembered that, in most countries of the world, universities are state-established and state-managed, and, despite the rising tide of national concern about student losses due to emotional distress, compete poorly for attention, funds, and staffing. Even in the best organized institutions of higher education in the most advanced nations, the mental health care of students has remained low in the national priorities for programming. University students still tend to be considered a select, even elitist, group receiving special opportunities and privileges, and are expected to maintain themselves in their academic careers ("sink or swim") without special help. Campus radicalism has served, furthermore, to raise the level of anti-intellectualism in some lands, particularly in governmental circles; and this quality of negativism has been reflected in a resistance to needed change in university structures.

COMMENTARIES ON STUDENT UNREST AND UNIVERSITY MENTAL HEALTH SERVICES

It would be appropriate to close this paper with comment on an aspect of student expression to which university mental health workers in recent years have been particularly sensitive: the politicization of the campus. This expression has appeared in varying strengths at different points, but there is agreement that it has been stronger and faster in development in countries outside of the United States and Canada. In a recent French poll (*Le Figaro*, March 10, 1972), for example, it was noted that 53% of the canvassed French youth felt drawn toward those who contested present-day society, and even a larger percentage stated that there could be no improvement in the lot of the French people without a "profound transformation of French society [*New York Times*,

March 11, 1972, p. 3]." Somewhat similar reports, descriptive of direct-action student activism, have had reference to campus situations and climates all over the world. The international scope of the "unrest" is well illustrated in the following reports: *New York Times*, March 1, 1971, pp. 1, 14 (France); March 9, 1971, pp. 39, 73 (Italy); August 28, 1971, p. 6 (Kuwait); October 4, 1971, pp. 1, 18 (the Philippines); January 18, 1972, p. 11 (Spain); and March 17, 1972, p. 11 (South Korea); *Argus*, July 10, 1971, pp. 1, 8 (Uganda); *Daily Nation*, July 21, 1971, p. 1 (Kenya); and *Times* (London), January 1, 1972, p. 4 (Yugoslavia). Also, see Olson, *et al.*, 1970, for relevant information on the Netherlands, Great Britain, India, Thailand, and Latin America. There are no hard data to connect ideological student movements with university mental health services, but points of view among the latter's professional staffs have not been lacking. Douady in France (1970) has already remarked on the negativism of radical student groups to the presumed "repressive psychology" induced into academic health service by the university "establishment." Further assessments were proffered by two key individuals in western Europe, as follows:

> It has been noted by us that these two sequential dynamic aspects, creative and inactive, in the phenomenon of protest (which has incorporated expressions of notable violence) may correspond from a psychological point of view to the characteristic oscillation in the behavior of some students who are confronted with the needed opportunity to use the Mental Hygiene Service. In the moments of greatest promise of the (Student) Movement, it seemed that many students succeeded in sublimating their personal problems in the creative sweep of new group values—for which reasons their rapport with the psychiatrist did not appear either specifically justifiable or valid in any manner. On the other hand, when the students collectively underwent the inevitable crisis of program reconstruction, the psychological ten-

sions of many participating students reappeared, which were no longer manageable within the framework of the Movement nor resolvable in charismatic experiences of group transcendance. In this latter circumstance, among numbers of students, there was a turning toward psychiatric assistance and a willingness to assign a therapeutic value to individual face-to-face meetings with the professional staff [Frighi, 1970, University of Rome].

The political roles taken by neurotically bound individuals in revolutions, and particularly in pseudorevolutionary youth movements, are demonstrations of the way in which such movements can assimilate clinically disturbed personalities. What is of interest to us is the upsurge of infantile patterns among individuals at a time of collective unrest; individual conflicts, individual alienations, tend to be discharged into a universe of conflict with the social system, with a rejection of all traditional concepts of work, performance, and authority, and with an accompanying development of a utopian fantasy. Under these circumstances, student unrest does not exist solely in a political context, but rather serves to some degree for the direct satisfaction of impulses and unrestrained discharge of aggression, finding justification, security, and superego transfer in the collective group. The aggressive hyperactivity, the demonstration of narcissistic omnipotence, prove, in an analytic sense, to be a defense strategy of personal helplessness and ego weakness, often alloyed with masochistic tendencies and latent homosexual strivings [Ziolko, 1970, Free University of Berlin].

REFERENCES

Alanen, Y. O., Holmström, R., Hagglund, V., Karlsson, K. W., Tienari, P., Vauhkonen, K., Savonen, K., Hirvas, J., & Marin, M. The mental health of Finnish university students: A psychiatric study of freshmen. *Social Psychiatry*, 1968, *3*, 60–65.

American Psychiatric Association, Committee on Academic Education. *Mental health practices in colleges and universities.* 1954.

Blaine, G. B., Jr., & McArthur, C. C. *Emotional problems of the student.* (2nd ed.) New York: Appleton-Century-Crofts, 1971.

Bloch, C. The "Service D'Aide Psychologique aux Etudiants" of the Free University of Brussels. In S. Pearlman (Ed.), *University mental health: International perspectives.* New York: Author, 1970.

Bloch, C., & Rapoport-Schoonbroodt, L. Special problems of individual psychotherapy with students during the examination period. In S. Pearlman (Ed.), *University mental health: International perspectives.* New York: Author, 1970.

Bloom, B. L. Characteristics of campus community mental health programs in Western United States—1969. *Journal of the American College Health Association*, 1970a, *18*, 196–200.

Bloom, B. L. Current issues in the provision of campus community mental health services. *Journal of the American College Health Association*, 1970b, *18*, 257–264.

Bouchal, M., Jaroš, M., & Kotulán, J. Living conditions and neuroticism in university students. *Acta Facultatis Medicae Universitatis Brunensis* (Brno, Czechoslovakia), 1967, *33*, 59–84.

Bouchal, M., & Jaroš, M. Neuroticism among medical school students in Czechoslovakia. In S. Pearlman (Ed.), *University mental health: International perspectives.* New York: Author, 1970.

Cass, W. A. *Personnel policies as applied to universities and college counseling center staff.* Pullman, Wash.: Washington State University, 1961.

Claramunt, F. Mental health and psychotherapy of students in Spain 1968. In H.-U. Ziolko (Ed.), *Psychologi-*

cal disorders among students. Stuttgart: Georg Thieme Verlag, 1969. Pp. 279–284.

Claramunt, F. Student mental health services in Spain. In S. Pearlman (Ed.), *University mental health: International perspectives.* New York: Author, 1970.

Congdon, R. C., & Lothrop, W. W. *Survey of college counseling practices in the United States.* Durham, N.H.: University of New Hampshire, 1963.

Davy, B. W. The sources and prevention of mental ill-health in university students. *Proceedings of the Royal Society of Medicine,* 1960, *53*(9), 764–769.

Davy, B. W. The disappointed undergraduate. *British Medical Journal,* 1957, *2,* 547–551.

Douady, D. Protection of the mental health of students in France. In S. Pearlman (Ed.), *University mental health: International perspectives.* New York: Author, 1970.

Farnsworth, D. L. *Mental health in college and university.* Cambridge, Mass.: Harvard University Press, 1957.

Frighi, L. The mental hygiene service of the University of Rome. In S. Pearlman (Ed.), *University mental health: International perspectives.* New York: Author, 1970.

Fry, C. C., & Rostow, E. A. *Mental health in college.* New York: Commonwealth Fund, 1942.

Funkenstein, D. H. (Ed.) *The student and mental health: An international view.* Cambridge, Mass.: Riverside Press, 1959.

Funkenstein, D. H., & Wilkie, G. H. *Student mental health: An annotated bibliography, 1936–1955.* London: World Federation for Mental Health, 1956.

Gedeon, S. M. Mental health services in Greek universities. In S. Pearlman (Ed.), *University mental health: International perspectives.* New York: Author, 1970.

Gerard, K., Jaroszynski, J., Ostaszewska, J., Flatau-Smulczynska, J., Stankiewicz, D., Uminska, A., & Wyosinska, T. An attempt to estimate the incidence of mental disturbance among students in schools of higher education. In S. Pearlman (Ed.), *University mental health: International perspectives.* New York: Author, 1970.

German, G. A. Mental health and mental illness in Eastern Africa. Paper presented at the staff conference of the New York Medical College, Department of Psychiatry, New York City, November, 1970.

German, G. A., & Arya, O. P. Psychiatric morbidity amongst a Uganda student population. *British Journal of Psychiatry,* 1969, *115,* 1323–1329.

Ginsburg, E. L. *The college and student health, based on the Fourth National Conference on health in colleges.* New York: National Tuberculosis Assn., 1955.

Group for the Advancement of Psychiatry, Committee on Academic Education. *The role of psychiatrists in colleges and universities.* (Rev. ed.) New York: GAP, 1957, No. 17.

Group for the Advancement of Psychiatry, Committee on the College Student. *The college experience: A focus for psychiatric research.* New York: GAP, 1962, No. 52.

Gundle, S., & Kraft, A. Mental health programs in American colleges and universities. *Bulletin of the Menninger Clinic,* 1956, *20,* 57–69

Holmström, R. Student mental health in Finland. In S. Pearlman (Ed.), *University mental health: International perspectives.* New York: Author, 1970.

International Student Service (later the World University Service). *Problems of student health: Report on an experts' conference held at Haslev, Denmark, April 20–27, 1949.* Geneva: ISS, 1949.

Ironside, W. The incidence of psychiatric illness in a group of New Zealand medical students. *Journal of the American College Health Association,* 1966, *15* (1), 50–53.

Ishicawa, K. Two-step method interview and the future of the students' mental health. *Bulletin of the Japanese*

National Association for Mental Health, Nos. 106–107, April, 1967. (In Japanese, but summarized in English by Yeh, E.-k., 1967.)

Kidd, C. B. Psychiatric morbidity among students. *British Journal of Preventive and Social Medicine,* 1965, *19* (4), 143–150.

Kidd, C. B., & Caldbeck-Meenan, J. A comparative study of psychiatric morbidity among students at two different universities. *British Journal of Psychiatry,* 1966, *112* (no. 482), 57–64.

Lancet (England), 1967, 1(No. 7485), 888–889; also 1967, 1(No. 7480), 34–35, and *British Medical Journal,* 1967, (No. 5550), 457–458.

Lucas, C. J., & Linken, A. Student mental health: A survey of developments in the United Kingdom. In S. Pearlman (Ed.), *University mental health: International perspectives.* New York: Author, 1970.

MacHaffie, R. A., & Nelson, E. L. Student health services in Scandinavia and their relationships to social medicine programs: Report of a study in Denmark, Norway, and Sweden. *Journal of the American College Health Association,* 1969, *17*(4), 296–301.

Malleson, N. *Papers of the International Association of Universities,* 1958, No. 3, pp. 57ff.

Nugent, F. A., & Pareis, E. N. *Survey—present practices in college counseling centers.* Bellingham, Wash.: Western Washington State College, 1965.

Olson, E. H., Wrenn, C. G., Johnson, W. F., & Bentley, J. C. Symposium on student response to authority. *Journal of College Student Personnel,* 1970, *11*(2), 83–93.

Pearlman, S. College mental health. In M. Siegel (Ed.), *The counseling of college students.* New York: The Free Press, 1968. Pp. 241–282.

Pearlman, S. *College mental health: a reference guide to the literature, 1919-1966.* Brooklyn, N. Y.: Author, 1966.

Pearlman, S. (Ed.) *University mental health: International perspectives.* New York: Author, 1970.

Pirozynski, T., Pirozynski, M., Gottlieb, H., & Taler, A. Some aspects of psychiatric assistance for students. In S. Pearlman (Ed.), *University mental health: International perspectives.* New York: Author, 1970.

Robbins, W. T. 1962 survey of mental health programs in colleges. In Pacific Coast Health Association, *Proceedings of the 26th annual meeting.* San Diego: PCHA, 1963.

Shimazaki, T., Takahashi, T., Miyamoto, T., & Takahashi, R. Mental health in college community: I. Students who left school because of mental disorders. *Bulletin of the Tokyo Dental and Medical University,* 1966, *13,* 311–318.

Srole, L., Langner, T. S., Michael, S. T., Opler, M. K., & Rennie, T. A. C. *Mental health in the metropolis: The midtown Manhattan study.* New York: McGraw-Hill, 1962.

Still, R. J. Preliminary report on a ten year survey of the mental health of students. *Proceedings of the 11th Conference of the British Student Health Association,* 1959, 33–49.

Vali-Wohl, A., & Hut, Tj. H. The mental care of students in the Netherlands. In S. Pearlman (Ed.), *University mental health: International perspectives.* New York: Author, 1970.

van de Voorde, H. Student mental health care in the Belgian universities. In S. Pearlman (Ed.), *University mental health: International perspectives.* New York: Author, 1970.

Vauhkonen, K., Alanen, Y. O., Enckell, M., Holmström, R., Karlsson, K. W., Stewen, A., Savonen, K., Hirvas, J., & Marin, M. The mental health of Finnish university students: A psychiatric study of a random sample of third and fourth year students. *Folia Psychiatrica Aboensia,* 1969, *1,* 1–16.

Wedge, B. M. (Ed.) *Psychosocial problems of college men.* New Haven: Yale University Press, 1958.

Whittington, H. G. *Psychiatry on the college campus.* New York: International Universities Press, 1963.

World Federation for Mental Health. *Bulletin*, Winter, 1970/71, 4–5.

World Federation for Mental Health. *Public health, education, and mental hygiene: Proceedings of the nineteenth annual meeting, Praha, July, 1966.* Geneva: WFMH, 1967.

World Health Organization. *University health services: Fourteenth report of the WHO expert committee on professional and technical education of medical and auxiliary personnel.* Technical Report Series, No. 320. Geneva: WHO, 1967.

World Health Organization, Regional Office for Europe. *Student health services. Report on a symposium convened by the Regional Office for Europe of the World Health Organization, Cracow, Poland, 15–20 April, 1966.* Copenhagen: WHO, 1967.

World University Service. *Problems of student health in Southeast Asia: Report of an experts' conference held at Singapore, Malaya, 28th March–4th April 1951.* Geneva: WUS, 1951.

World University Service. *A study of university health services based on a world survey to which 40 countries responded.* Part I. Geneva: WUS, 1955.

World University Service. *European conference of experts on student mental health, Schloss Munchenwiler bei Murten, Switzerland, August 21–27, 1961.* Geneva: WUS, 1963.

World University Service. *Student health in Asia: Report of the WUS Asian conference of experts on student health, Peradeniya, Ceylon, April 22–29, 1962.* Geneva: WUS, 1962.

World University Service. *Student health in Asia: Report of the third WUS Asian student health conference, Chiengmai, Thailand, April 21–29, 1966.* Geneva: WUS, 1966.

Wright-Short, F. W. The emotional problems of undergraduates. *Medical Journal of Australia*, 1967, *1*(18), 913–914.

Yale University, Department of Psychiatry and Mental Hygiene, Division of Student Mental Hygiene. *Publications on college mental hygiene.* (Unpublished manuscript.) New Haven: Yale University, undated.

Yeh, E.-k. Student mental health—Services and epidemiology in Taiwan (Republic of China). In S. Pearlman (Ed.), *University mental health: International perspectives.* New York: Author, 1970.

Yeh, E.-k., Chu, H.-m., & Ko, Y.-h. Some psychiatric findings of the college students in Taiwan. Revision (1967) of paper presented at the 18th annual meeting of the World Federation for Mental Health, Bangkok, Thailand, November, 1965.

Ziolko, H.-U. (Ed.) *Psychische störungen bei studenten.* [Psychological disorders among students.] Stuttgart: Georg Thieme Verlag, 1969.

Ziolko, H.-U. The situation of the student advisory offices in West Germany and West Berlin. In S. Pearlman (Ed.), *University mental health: International perspectives.* New York: Author, 1970.

Part III

PROGRAMS IN ACTION

8. The Peer Program: An Experiment in Humanistic Education

BEN C. FINNEY

This is a brief account of a successful experiment in humanistic education, the Peer Program[1] at San Jose State College. It demonstrated that students can be taught to understand themselves and others in deeply meaningful ways, that they can be helped to change their behavior and their feelings about themselves, that they can be taught to develop warm, honest relationships with their peers, and that the loneliness of an impersonal college can be eased. Furthermore, participating students learned abstract, intellectual concepts at the same time they were learning to feel and react on a very personal level, and these experiences were combined in their education in an atmosphere of trust with a professor with whom they had developed a warm relationship.

The Peer Program, which operated for five years with about five hundred students in total, showed that these goals can be achieved within the structure of regular col-

[1]The name "Peer Program" was chosen to indicate that the peer relationships were the central focus; the similarity in name with the program of Betty Berzon was accidental.

lege classes without extensive special funding or facilities; the project was financed solely from one half-time teaching and one half-time counseling position.

The program was organized around a "Tribe" of eighty students supervised by a "Peer Professor" (the author) who taught the core psychology class to the fifty new members on a half-time teaching position and who spent a considerable part of his half-time counseling position counseling Peer students. During the five years I always had one continuing Tribe, one year I handled an additional Tribe, and one year three other Counseling Center psychologists each led a Tribe.[2]

The Peer Tribe was a community of students, made up of new members recruited without restrictions from the entering freshmen class and about thirty continuing members. The tribe was broken down into eight "Clans" of ten members each who met twice weekly as encounter groups. Two student "Grems" or "*Gr*eatly *e*xperienced *m*ember*s*" served as participant-leaders and met weekly with the Peer Professor to report and discuss their Clans. The Tribe met monthly, as part of some extra social activities, and also at the two mandatory weekend marathons each semester.

During the time the Peer Program was in operation —it was stopped in 1969 because of the severe budget crisis in California Colleges—it gave these students an experience in humanistic education oriented toward personal growth. Almost all of the people directly involved in the program reported that it was meaningful and effective.

Originally we had hoped to set up a formal experiment, but in the process of working out an effective system we were constantly making changes, and the practical difficulties made an experiment impossible. We believe the structure, techniques, and philosophy that have evolved,

[2]These psychologists were John Borghi, Thornton Hooper, and David Stoker.

however, have been shown to be practical and effective and that these could be used in other schools.

RECRUITMENT AND COMMON CLASSES

Entering freshmen of any major were invited to join the program during orientation week. In addition, we accepted some other students who had heard about the program from their friends. Fifty new members who would agree to take the three-unit psychology class and pay $25.00 for the marathon and social expenses were recruited each year. For three years we preregistered the entering Peer Freshmen in three common classes, including Psychology, which were required General Education courses. Preregistration provided an incentive to join, and the students liked knowing the other students in several of their classes. They felt they were more comfortable speaking up in class and they did a good deal of studying together. They became very cohesive and would defend each other and challenge the professors; some professors found this an uncomfortable change and some liked the liveliness of the Peers. Administrative difficulties led us to drop the common classes, and although this did not have a significant effect on the Peer culture, we think common classes were worthwhile.

THE PEER CLASS

Fifty students took Exploratory Psychology, on a pass-fail basis; it met twice a week for an hour. In addition, they were required to meet twice a week with their Clans; the Clans all met at the same time in student apartments and were visited on a rotational basis.

Texts were used that focused on personality dynamics. Every other week students wrote essays on the assigned chapters, with the instructions that they were to take three main concepts of their own choice, discuss these

concepts intellectually, and relate them to their own experiences. We read the essays, wrote comments on them,
and encouraged the students to integrate the abstract
concepts with their own personal feelings. On alternate
weeks, they wrote an informal letter about themselves
and their feelings. We encouraged the students to pass the
letters and essays on to the Grems; Clan members not in
the class were required to write weekly letters to their
Clan Grem.

These letters and essays helped establish an emotional
bond between us, as well as keep us in touch with them.
The students wrote candid and trusting essays, and we
found we enjoyed reading them. It was general policy
within the Tribe that I was to be kept informed about
everything that went on. Hearing regularly from the
group leaders about the Clan meetings and reading the
essays and letters, I kept in close touch with the whole
Tribe and they felt reassured that I was watching for
difficulties and was available for help. When students
were feeling especially troubled I would see them individ-
ually in the Counseling Center.

The class meetings were very informal, and my lectures
were casual discussions of psychological dynamics, illustrated from my own clinical experiences; these they
found helped them think more deeply about themselves.
I also used encounter group exercises, and developed
some of my own. Frequently, I would pair them to discuss
some sensitive topic, such as sex or anger, and then have
them share some of their reactions with the group.

My relationship with them was warm and informal, and
I was direct in showing my affection—touching, embrac-
ing, and expressing my feelings openly. I deliberately
"modeled" a style of relating which became a part of the
Peer tradition; students said that they especially valued
learning how to give and take love and how to enjoy
nonsexual touching. When students became uneasy with
the possible sexual implications of physical contact, I encouraged them to be open with their discomfort, and

their frankness plus the reassurances from older Peers seemed to handle these anxieties.

By demonstrating honesty and candor and sharing my feelings, I tried to set an example of how to relate openly and intimately. I have carried this as far as exposing some of my most sensitive feelings, with tears and pain, in a marathon session with a Clan. The students responded deeply to this kind of relationship with a professor and gave me respect and affection.

THE CLANS

Every peer was assigned to one of eight Clans of ten members each. They were assigned at random but with an effort to maintain a balance of sexes and of new and old members. Students came to value the Clan approach to relationships—so unlike the exclusiveness of the fraternity system—where every person was considered important and worth knowing. In the Clans, the old members, who set the tone of open, frank discussions, and the two most experienced members were assigned the role of Grem. The Clans were visited in rotation, but provision was also made to respond to Clans that asked for help. Difficulties in the Clans were usually associated with their inability to deal with the fears and resentments of the Clan members. It was our impression that the Clans operated at a level equal to most professionally-led encounter groups.

In the Clans we played a very active role and the general style which we demonstrated was to be warm and supportive but to push for feelings, especially painful childhood feelings; I would often use some special techniques, such as "Say It Again" (Finney, 1971) and "Little Child Talk" (Finney, 1969a, 1969b). When a member got bruised it was usually because the Clan had tried to attack or challenge in an insensitive way. I did not encourage superficialities but pushed for strong emotions and catharsis, especially with tears. At the marathons we would have many dramatic "breakthroughs" of feeling, followed by much closeness and affection in the Clan.

GROUP LEADERS OR GREMS

The day-to-day leadership of the Clans was provided by the Grems. In the beginning, I recruited graduate students and other adults experienced in encounter groups for the role of Grem. Later, I gained confidence in the student leaders and selected students who had had at least a year in the Peers to work in pairs as Grems. Not all of the Grems functioned well, but some of the experienced ones became very skilled group leaders.

The role of the Grem was phrased as a "greatly experienced member" rather than as an "expert" or "therapist." They were to show the other members how to work by demonstrating it themselves. They were also the persons who kept trying to keep the group going well, and they served as my representatives, informing me of difficulties. The Grems picked up my style, which was pushy but with caring and gentleness, and they would bring students to my attention who needed individual interviews with me.

I met with the Grems weekly, and talked with them about their feelings, about their roles, and about the difficulties they were having; these meetings were more like encounter groups focused on feelings rather than case conferences.

MARATHONS

The most powerful and effective activity of the Peers was the weekend marathons twice each semester which-everyone was expected to attend. We met at a summer camp, each Clan bringing its own food and bedding. We met as a whole Tribe Friday evening from 8 to 11 p.m. doing a number of encounter exercises (Finney, 1970).

These exercises were powerful enough that there would be tears or strong feelings which set the tone for the subsequent individual Clan meetings. The Clans met separately and continuously until Saturday night. Sunday morning closing ceremonies, after a night's sleep, again brought the Tribe together. Some rituals were developed which heightened the mood, which was one of elation and love, and these became a tradition. One student described a marathon as follows:

> While in your Clan you begin to talk about your problems and feelings toward each other. You can show your feelings. You can cry or scream or do almost anything you want. Every time the people in the Clans get everything out in the open—by open I mean feelings—the Clan gets closer together; you begin to trust one another. You feel so full of love and happiness toward yourself and others it makes you feel like nothing can go wrong and the whole world isn't against you. That is what I feel anyway.

EVALUATION AND DISCUSSION

At the end of each year the students were asked to evaluate the program. As part of the evaluation a twenty-item questionnaire was included. For brevity, four items have been selected from one year, 1966, along with some narrative comments.

I feel more confident of being able to face and handle my personal problems.

Better 86%   Worse 0%   No Change 14%

> One thing I want to stress, especially to you, Ben, is how happy I am now. When I remember how badly I always felt when I first came in to see you and then compare it with now, I'm so grateful for the whole Peer trip.

I think I understand better how my past experience affects my present behavior.

Better 98%   Worse 0%   No Change 2%

Peers has given me confidence in myself because I have been able to reason certain factors out in a verbal way which helped a great deal. Peers does give me a sense of belonging to a collection of people striving to give and receive love, the essence of life. The process of growing up is extremely painful without anyone near to talk to. One idea that struck me as beautiful was that the thoughts that I think are not totally new and weird; they are thought by many persons.

I feel more aware of the feelings of others.

Better 88%   Worse 0%   No Change 12%

I feel I've gained a lot of awareness about myself and other people. I'm now sensitive to others, their needs, and what I can honestly give. I've become aware of a part of me that I've repressed and knew nothing about. I feel more like a person.

I am better able to express myself in groups.

Better 75%   Worse 0%   No Change 25%

I am much more at ease with group situations and I am much more open, and by the same sense I am much more open with myself. For the most part, my ties and relationships with all those around me are much deeper than before. I am more willing to listen and understand, much more open with myself and ready to show my feelings.

I believe the Peer experience produced some significant changes, aiding the natural growth processes and helping with some of the pain and frustration of college life.

The students consistently reported that they became more sensitive to themselves and others, were able to listen and understand more, and had deeper relationships with more honesty and more trusting. They felt increased security and less loneliness, along with more self-worth and more feelings of responsibility for their own actions. Furthermore, they reported that the Peer Program met some deep needs for a sense of belonging to a community that valued individuality rather than conformity, honest and close relationships rather than superficiality and appearances, and warmth and mutual support rather than competition and isolation. They said the program gave them increased insight into psychological dynamics and how their personal history had led them to be the persons they were. And they felt that their relationships changed with their family, friends, and themselves. The most consistent and frequently mentioned change was that they had learned to be more loving, giving and accepting affection through touch, words, and actions.

Not all the students shared these reactions, and some rejected the program as trying to force them into saying that they were sick and needed psychotherapy. A few felt that it upset them more than it helped them. I was not aware of more than a very few "psychiatric casualties," none severe. This is in contrast to Yalom and Lieberman's finding (1970) that 10% of students in 18 professionally-led encounter groups became more psychologically distressed from the group experience. One explanation is that I discouraged the leadership style of "aggressive stimulators," which produced the highest casualty rate, and fostered a style like the "love leader," which had the lowest. Also I kept close watch on the members and followed up with individual interviews whenever a student seemed disturbed or needful.

There were some difficulties and a few complaints from parents, but we had the enthusiastic support of Robert Clark, former President of San Jose State College, and the college administration stood very steady when we had difficulties.

We believe, first, that almost every student can benefit from this kind of "growth education." It is not just for the emotionally disturbed, nor do students have to be screened to exclude the "unstable" ones. The Peers included some "healthy" and some "troubled" students, but all of them were experiencing some personal pain and most of them found they could share and explore it in the Clans. Some did not like the Peer experience and about one-quarter of the students dropped out for various reasons at the end of the first semester. A few said they got their feelings bruised and the Peer Program was not helpful, but most found it a very rewarding experience.

Second, we believe that intellectual and cognitive education can be combined with growth in emotional understanding and with learning effective and rewarding ways of relating; these supplement each other and a college class is an appropriate place to combine them.

The third point is that the "student culture" is a powerful educational force which can work with or against the aims of academic education, and that a deliberate effort to shape it so that it supports learning and growth can succeed.

Fourth, students can learn to help each other, with the more experienced ones leading encounter groups, transmitting the culture, and helping the new ones gain the growth that the more experienced ones have already achieved; in turn older students develop from the experience of leadership, caring for others, as well as from their own continued personal exploration.

Fifth, a large group of students can be given a sustained growth experience—essentially what is offered in individual and group psychotherapy—with a limited amount of time from a professional psychologist. This kind of social organization offers a way of using our limited professional time to reach a much wider number of students.

The key to such a program is a network of intimate and enduring relationships. I established personal ties with all of the students and they formed attachments to me and to each other that continue over the years. They identified with me and the values I sponsored and "modeled" —which are the values of "humanistic psychology"—and these became a part of the Peer culture. A web of caring relationships developed and the Peers became like an extended family, especially among the Clan members.

We believe that we have developed a program which can meet some of the lacks in contemporary college education. It is our hope that other humanistically-oriented counselors and psychology professors will find this account intriguing enough that they will experiment with this kind of educational program. We will be pleased to share our experiences in more detail (Finney, 1970).

REFERENCES

Finney, B. C. The flower turn-on: A group technique. *Group Leaders Digest.* July, 1969a. Explorations Institute, P. O. Box 1254, Berkeley, Ca.

Finney, B. C. Let the little child talk: A new psychotherapeutic technique. *American Journal of Psychotherapy,* 1969b, *23,* 230–242.

Finney, B. C. The peer program: An extended report. Unpublished manuscript. 1970.

Finney, B. C. Say it again: An active therapy technique. Unpublished manuscript. 1971.

Yalom, I. D., and Lieberman, M. Encounter group casualties. Paper, Annual Meeting 1970, American Psychiatric Association.

9. Improving Mental Health Services on Western Campuses

A Regional Action Program

JAMES H. BANNING

The program, "Improving Mental Health Services on Western Campuses," was developed by the Mental Health and Related Areas Division of WICHE, the Western Interstate Commission for Higher Education. WICHE is a nonprofit agency created by the 13 western states to administer the Western Regional Education Compact which became operative in 1953. The Compact is an agreement among the states to cooperate in order to provide improved educational facilities and programs to meet the needs of the West. Working from a regional base gives programs an advantage in identifying problems common to many schools and in bringing a number of people together to work on the problems.

"Improving Mental Health Services on Western Campuses" had its genesis four years ago when it became apparent that WICHE might study two long-standing interests—mental health and higher education—where they intersect on the university campus. A preliminary survey was conducted throughout schools of higher education in the West (Bloom, 1970a, 1970b). The findings showed that while enrollments had significantly increased, growing more heterogeneous with proliferating problems, mental health services had remained relatively static in manpower, research and innovative programming, and evaluation.

Faced with clear evidence that improved mental health services were needed to meet current campus needs, WICHE obtained a grant from the Experimental and Special Training Branch of the National Institute of Mental Health which supports our three-year program to review campus mental health activities, identify and consider issues regarding these activities, and formulate strategies for change and for the development of innovative methods to improve the organization and delivery of mental health services on the campus community.

CONCEPTUAL FRAMEWORK FOR THE PROGRAM

The program hopes to bring the student development viewpoint in concert with the concepts of community mental health. This hope embraces the idea that students in higher education are involved in negotiating a number of tasks that relate directly to their personal development as well as to the growth of their mental health generally. This process is directly affected by the students' educational community environment. Because the role of mental health in higher education should be directed toward facilitating individual growth and development through community interventions as well as individual counseling, campus as community becomes the major conceptual backdrop for the program.

Despite the revolutionary impact the community mental health movement has had upon many segments of our society, it has had relatively little impact upon the organization and delivery of mental health services on campuses. It is astonishing and puzzling that only the faintest ripples have pushed into the campus community from so revolutionary a wave.

Much time could be expended in seeking reasons for this puzzling isolation. A key component would no doubt be the general stature of aloofness universities have historically maintained. And of equal importance, if not more so, is the traditional concept of *in loco parentis* the university has held to so firmly in years past. As parents we seldom look upon our offspring as groups or communities and are more likely to focus on interpersonal relationships where intrapsychic functioning and the dyadic relationships become paramount. Perhaps in acting *in loco parentis* our universities have taken a similar attitude, with the result that very few community mental health approaches have permeated into our systems of higher education.

Is the Campus a Community?

Certainly the average tourist driving past one of our college campuses would not recognize the campus as a community. The usual landmarks of a business section ringed by patterns of residential dwellings, shopping centers, and parks are not visible. The homogeneous exterior of the campus masks the fact that a community with centers of business, living, shopping, and recreation is thriving amid the clipped lawns, stately trees, and carefully planned complex of buildings. More importantly, the traditional sociological elements of a community—territorial entity, functional unity, and sense of a shared common destiny as it applies to education (Howe, 1964)—are present. And like communities everywhere, the campus community evolves its systems by which to accomplish various functions. Admission systems, registration systems, living systems, and administrative systems are only a few which exist in this community (Pervin, 1967).

Nor is the campus community immune to the conflicts and stresses common to other communities. The sources of problems are many. Some problems originate with individual community members, some from groups within the community, some from the community and its operational systems, and some from the frictions of each component interacting upon the others.

STATUS OF COMMUNITY MENTAL HEALTH MODEL ON CAMPUS

Given that the campus is a community, what would be the model for a campus community mental health program? Drawing from literature on the community mental health model as applied to the campus community (Barger *et al.*, 1966; Larson *et al.*, 1969; Reifler *et al.*, 1967; Havens, 1970; Nidorf, 1970; Bloom, 1070b; Reid, 1070), the following model may serve as a guide for the campus community:

1. Community participation in the development, delivery, and evaluation of services.
2. Intervention at both community and individual levels with a wide array of intervention strategies.
3. Emergency programming.
4. Consultative and educational programming with a heavy focus upon preventive intervention strategies.
5. Research and evaluation.

Using these brief statements as the cornerstones of our model, how are the campus communities in the West sizing up?

Regarding community participation in the development, delivery, and evaluation of services, our impressions and observations are that community participation is notably lacking. Members of campus communities are only occasionally assessed regarding needs. Perusal of our survey data on outreach programming has shown that programs usually were developed as the result of staff interest and needs. This means many programs may be serving the staff rather than serving the community.

Community participation in the delivery of services is also notably lacking. In a recent program survey (Banning and Aulepp, 1971), only eight mental health facilities out of 155 reported using paraprofessionals in the delivery of services. These paraprofessionals ranged from undergraduate students to members of the community at large. This statistic becomes even more striking when compared with the survey results that show 17 percent of these campuses have mental health services organized and administered by students. It can be assumed from this information that students are interested and possess skills in the delivery of services, but this fact has not yet been reflected by the staffing patterns of university-operated campus mental health facilities.

Community participation in the evaluation of services is also slow in coming. While a few centers engage in some type of formal evaluation from the community, most do not. But, again students are beginning to take the initiative. A growing trend appears to be the development of student advocacy programs to look at the services supposedly designed for them.

The second cornerstone, intervention at both community and individual levels with a wide array of intervention strategies, has not received wide attention. The primary intervention strategy for campus mental health facilities in the West is individual and small group counseling. The survey data showed facilities spend from 60 to 78 percent of their staff time in these two activity areas. Other activities such as consultation, mental health education, preventive and outreach programming, research, testing, training, evaluation, and crisis services receive from one to nine percent of staff time. This uniformity in intervention strategies is distressing because it flies in the face of the contrasts which exist among the institutions of higher education in the West, their educational emphasis, geographical and physical environments, and student populations. It would seem that community-oriented influences have had little bearing upon the programs offered by the campus mental health facility.

A more positive trend is seen in the development of the model's third cornerstone, emergency programming. Recipients of the survey were asked to indicate whether the following types of programs were functioning on their campus: (1) crisis service or walk-in procedure during normal university hours; (2) 24-hour crisis intervention program or after-hours and weekend emergency service; (3) telephone emergency service, "rap line," "hot line," etc.; (4) an emergency service organized and administered by students; and (5) other services not covered ty the above categories.

Ninety-three percent of the campuses responding had at least one of the five types of crisis programs operating. By far the most predominant program was the walk-in service during regular university hours. Nearly half of the campuses, however, offer some type of around-the-clock coverage. It can also be noted from the data that the larger the school the more likely that telephone emergency service is available. Likewise, larger campuses are more prone to have a student-administered crisis service.

There are hopeful signs indicating movement in the area of our fourth cornerstone, consultation and education programming with a heavy focus upon preventive intervention strategies. While little staff time is devoted to these activities in comparison to individual and small group counseling, many of the campus mental health facilities are beginning to initiate more programming in this area. Consultation and education still appear, however, to be focused on the individual rather than the community or its subsystems. Consultative activities in residence halls and drug education programs appear to be the primary thrusts. The status of facilities' efforts in research and education, the model's final cornerstone, is low. Little staff time is spent in these areas. Perhaps the current theme of accountability in higher education will give impetus to these activities.

In summary, the status of a campus community mental health model can best be described as having a potential to move, but having a rather large challenge ahead.

CHALLENGE FOR CAMPUS MENTAL HEALTH FACILITIES

To meet the challenge of a community focus, campus mental health facilities must face the essential question: What is the facility's role in relation to the systems operating in the campus community? Among the myriad of systems functioning on campuses, the mental health center generally has been relegated to the role of pacification and maintenance of the status quo. The center has responded to the assignment by focusing its activities on working with individuals so that they can return to the educational community and make the necessary adjustments. In short, by assuming this role mental health centers have accommodated to an uneducational environment. Little activity, or perhaps even little thought, is given to applying the behavioral science skills housed in the center to bring about constructive environmental change. By declining to use its skill and knowledge in this manner the center, in fact, allows an uneducational environment to continue. But to incorporate the community mental health model's concern for social and environmental well-being evokes emotions from both the center's personnel and other campus administrators. It is at this point that feelings become tender and efforts hesitant. The issue becomes embroiled in a discussion of the validity and appropriateness of campus mental health centers as agents of change within their communities.

People in the field have begun to speak out on the issue. Their ideas lend reason to the debate and spur the cloistered campus mental health centers to break from tradition and become active participants in their community's life. Nidorf has urged campus centers to go beyond individual care and start treating the community's dysfunctions noting:

> to prevent personal and social ills requires social change of a qualitative nature—not just quantitative treatment additions. Unfortunately, in any social institution, qualitative changes are hard to come by. The change agent, by its very nature, must be political. It must be able to influence the many dimensions of vested interest maintaining the status quo. An ideal model for such an agent—a model that has been tested and proven effective—is the comprehensive mental health agency [1970, p. 21].

Farnsworth has challenged psychiatrists to bite the political bullet and become true to the principles of their profession. In his words:

> accusations of exhibiting political bias, having a moral point of view, or being a social engineer must be expected. Psychiatrists generally, and college psychiatrists particularly, must have *some* point of view if their efforts are not to be futile. . . . The bias of the college psychiatrist is explicitly toward freedom, independence, integrity, sincerity, humane attitudes, and the development of sound and effective methods for coping with the conflicts and ambiguities common to all who strive to improve the human situation. To sit idly by without attempting to direct social change in the direction of improvement rather than disintegration in the good human relations is an abduction of wisdom and common sense and unworthy of the traditions of psychiatry [1970, pp. 471–2].

These gentlemen have eloquently stated that the urgent need for campus mental health centers to become agents of change within their community is worth the troubles that will be encountered.

PROSPECTS FOR THE FUTURE

As "Improving Mental Health Services on Western Campuses" continues its efforts, we witness an increasing interest in the community approach. Response to the program's newsletter and workshop presentations at professional meetings denotes growing awareness of the model's usefulness to campus, while the program's task force work underscores campus needs for a community focus.

We believe the model stimulates interest because its components strike a responsive chord with a number of concerns on campus today. Concern for student participation in all phases of campus life fits well with the community participation cornerstone of the model. Environment and human ecology are of increasing concern generally. A community approach can speak to these issues as it moves toward a more socio-environmental explanation of student stress with greater emphasis upon disordered environments than disordered students. Concern for personal growth is taking on greater significance as more and more students feel the complexities of society and the campus rob them of their individuality. The prevention component of the community model aims at providing growth opportunities and experiences for students as well as removing unwarrented environmental stress.

We feel prospects for future programming within the concept of community look promising. As the campus community grows more reflective of the society in which it lives, the greater the need will be for campus mental health facilities to move toward community responsiveness and leadership. The resulting impact will benefit the entire campus community.

REFERENCES

Banning, J. H., & Aulepp, L. *University community mental health services survey.* Reported in: *Salary data for campus mental health professionals in the West, Monograph No. 1,* and *Staffing patterns of campus mental health facilities in the West, Monograph No. 2,* and *Program activities and student utilization of campus mental health facilities in the West, Monograph No. 3,* Western Interstate Commission for Higher Education, Boulder, Colorado, 1971.

Barger, B., Hall, E., & Larson, E. A. Preventive action in college mental health. *Journal of the American College Health Association,* 1966, *15,* 80–93.

Bloom, B. L. Characteristics of campus community mental health programs in Western United States—1969. *Journal of the American College Health Association,* 1970a, *18,* 196–200.

Bloom, B. L. Current issues in the provision of campus community mental health services. *Journal of the American College Health Association,* 1970b, *18,* 257–264.

Farnsworth, D. L. College mental health and social change. *Annals of Internal Medicine,* 1970, *73,* 467–473.

Havens, J. Beyond the clinical cocoon: Community mental health in the university. *Journal of the American College Health Association,* 1970, *19,* 101–104.

Howe, L. P. The concept of the community: Some implications for the development of community psychiatry. In L. Bellak (Ed.), *Handbook of Community Psychiatry,* New York: Grune and Stratton, 1964.

Larson, E. A., Barger, B., & Cahoon, S. N. College mental health programs: A paradigm for comprehensive community mental health centers. *Community Mental Health Journal,* 1969, *5,* 461–467.

Nidorf, L. J. Community mental health model applied to student personnel work. *Journal of College Student Personnel,* 1970, *11,* 19–27.

Pervin, L. The college as a social system. *Journal of Higher Education,* 1967, *37,* 317–322.

Reid, K. Community mental health on the college campus. *Hospital and Community Psychiatry*, December 1970, 23–25.
Reifler, C. B., Liptzin, M. B., & Fox, J. T. College psychiatry as public health psychiatry. *American Journal of Psychiatry*, 1967, *124*, 662–671.

10. Counseling Outreach Programs on the College Campus

WESTON H. MORRILL
JAMES H. BANNING

Many counselors are no longer content with waiting in their offices for students with problems to come to them. They recognize a responsibility not only for the relatively few students who come to them, but also for the many students who have not found their way to the counseling office. Counselors want to extend their role to the prevention of problems and the promotion of development rather than being concerned solely with the remediation of problems after they have developed (Bloom, 1971; Danskin, 1965; Levy, 1969; Morrill & Hurst, 1971; Morrill, Ivey, & Oetting, 1968). Programs of this kind have been called outreach programs and are becoming an important function of counseling on college campuses.

This investigation was supported in part by the following P.H.S. Research Grants from the National Institute of Mental Health: #1 R01 MH18007–01A1 from the Applied Research Branch and #MH12419 from the Experimental and Special Training Branch.

209

THE 1968 SURVEY OF OUTREACH PROGRAMS

In the summer of 1968 a questionnaire was mailed to 635 counseling center administrators in the United States to determine to what extent counseling centers were involved in outreach programs (Morrill & Oetting, 1970). The questionnaire provided a check list of twenty-six extratraditional or outreach type programs, and the counseling director responded by checking programs in which his center was involved. Sixty-three percent or 397 questionnaires were returned. Of these, 71 centers indicated that they were not involved in any outreach activities. The remaining 326 administrators checked an average of 9.6 programs on the check list. Although there were a sizeable group of centers that were not involved in outreach activities, the authors concluded that there was a trend toward more participation in this type of activity.

A REDEFINITION OF OUTREACH

In the first survey, outreach was defined as those activities which involve a counselor in interactions with relevant populations in locations other than his counseling office. A more recent definition of outreach is based on the nature of the counselor's intervention rather than on the location of these interventions (Morrill, Oetting, & Hurst, 1972). They defined counseling interventions as "the broad range of counselor behaviors which are designed to produce changes in clients, groups, or institutions [p. 1]." A model was presented which allowed the categorization and classification of counseling programs along three dimensions. These three dimensions were:

1. The *target of the intervention*, which referred to interventions aimed at (a) the individual, (b) his primary group(s), (c) his associational groups, or (d) the institutional or societal groups that influence his behavior.

2. The *purpose of the intervention,* referring to whether the purpose of the interventions is of (a) a remedial nature, (b) a preventative nature, or (c) a developmental nature and not involving a problem orientation.
3. The *method of intervention,* whether direct or indirect. That is, whether the counselor is (a) directly involved in initiating and implementing the intervention, or (b) if he is indirectly involved through consultation, training of others, or use of media.

FIGURE 1

Counseling Dimensions Contrasting Outreach and Traditional Program Areas

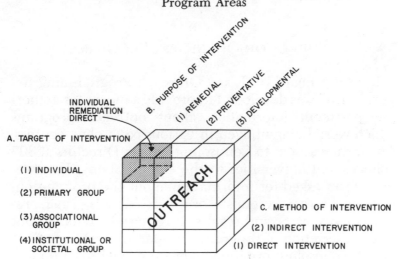

Figure 1 presents these dimensions and indicates the definition of outreach. Those interventions which are not solely individual, remedial, direct interventions are defined as outreach. As indicated by Morrill, Oetting, & Hurst (1972), the individual-remedial-direct intervention cell of the diagram represents the cornerstone of most counseling center programs. Examples of this type of program include traditional individual counseling or therapy which employs face-to-face contact between the professional and the individual. Since traditionally most counseling centers have spent the majority of their professional resources in this this area, outreach is defined as any program that moves from this cell on the model along any one or combination of the dimensions. For example, programs that are aimed at creating changes in the groups or institutions that affect the individual rather than changing the individual himself would be classed as outreach. Similarly, programs designed to prevent problems or promote positive development rather than to merely attempt repairs of problems already developed would be classed as outreach programs.

A SURVEY OF OUTREACH PROGRAMS[1]

In the spring of 1971, an "Outreach Programming Report Form" was developed to provide a means for gathering pertinent information about outreach programs which were being utilized in various counseling centers. The form was sent to Counseling Center Directors at 303 colleges and universities in the United States. The two-page form asked for information about the program objectives, target groups, program details, staff requirements, costs, and results. It required a detailed but brief description of programs in operation. Descriptions of 220 counseling programs were received from 96 colleges and universities. These programs were classified according to the model developed by Morrill, Oetting, & Hurst (1972) described earlier.

Table 1 presents a distribution of programs on the first dimension, the *target* of the intervention. Of the 220 pro-

[1]A more detailed report of this survey has been published in the following: Morrill, W. H., and Banning, J. H. (Ed.), *Counseling outreach: a survey of practices.* Western Interstate Commission for Higher Education, 1973.

grams, 183 or 83 percent were aimed at interventions with the individual. Eighteen of the programs (8 percent) were designed to intervene with the organized (associational) groups to which individuals belong. Fourteen or 6 percent of the programs were designed to deal with individuals' primary or strong identification groups such as family. The remaining five or 2 percent of the programs were aimed at interventions with the institutions that influence individuals.

TABLE 1

Distribution of Counseling Programs along the Target of Intervention Dimension

Target of Intervention	Number of Programs	Percent of Total
Individual	183	83.2
Primary group	14	6.4
Associational group	18	8.2
Institution or society	5	2.3

Table 2 presents the distribution of counseling programs along the *purpose* of intervention dimension. On this dimension, the purpose of 86 or 40 percent of the programs was to remediate existing problems. Seventy-two or 33 percent of the programs were designed to prevent problems from occurring. The remaining 59 or 27 percent of the programs were of a developmental nature, having as their purpose promoting positive growth rather than preventing or providing remedial help with problems.

Table 3 presents the distribution of counseling programs along the *method* of intervention dimension. This dimension indicates whether the counselor is directly involved in initiating and implementing the intervention or indirectly involved through consultation, training of others, or use of media. Of the 220 programs, 144 or 66 percent were classified as direct and 74 or 34 percent as indirect. In response to questions about the staff required for the programs, the respondents indicated that 128 or 58 percent of the programs utilized only professionals in their operation. Forty of the programs (18 percent) utilized both professionals and paraprofessionals or students. Thirty-eight of the programs (17 percent) utilized professionals as supervisors with the actual program implementation by paraprofessionals and students.

TABLE 2

Distribution of Counseling Programs along the Purpose of
Intervention Dimension

Purpose of Intervention	Number of Programs	Percent of Total
Remediation	89	40
Prevention	72	33
Development	59	27

Forty-seven of the 220 programs (21 percent) were classified as individual, remedial, direct intervention. That is, the target of the program was on creating change in the individual, the purpose of the change was to remediate an existing problem, and the intervention was made directly by the professional. Thus, even though the survey specifically requested descriptions of programs which were of an outreach nature, 21 percent of the programs reported do not fit the definition of outreach programs.

Table 4 presents a summary of the programs by content area. The greatest number of programs were classified under field and community counseling and consultation programs. These programs involved the counselor moving out of the office to counsel or consult in a variety of campus and community locations. The majority of these programs had to do with the counselor making his services available in various community locations such as residence halls, deans' offices, student unions, student health services, and community service agencies. Several of these programs involved merely doing individual counseling in different settings although some included a consultative role as well.

TABLE 3
Distribution of Counseling Programs along the Method of
Intervention Dimension

Method of Intervention	Number of Programs	Percent of Total
Direct	145	66
Indirect	75	34

Table 5 presents a summary of how the need for programs was determined. Almost half of the programs were developed because of the interest and the perceived need for the program by counseling directors and counselors. A large number of the programs were developed in response to requests by groups and individuals outside the counseling center such as students, faculty, and administrators.

SUMMARY AND DISCUSSION

In addition to the results of the survey, there is evidence which indicates that counselors and counseling centers are becoming more and more involved in outreach programs. There have been an increasing number of articles and convention programs dealing with outreach concepts. The National Institute of Mental Health recently funded major projects at Colorado State University and the Western Interstate Commission for Higher Education to study outreach programs and the delivery of mental health programs on the college campus.

To date, the majority of counseling center programs have been aimed at the individual and their purpose is remedial. As indicated earlier, this is the cornerstone of counselor training and practice. The potential impact of the counselor is limited by exclusive reliance on this approach. The waiting-list problem is a common counseling center concern. Efforts need to be made to maximize

TABLE 4
Summary and Rank of Programs by Content of Program

Rank	Content of Programs	Number of Programs	Percent of Total
1.5	Field and community counseling and consultation	24	11
1.5	Crisis intervention and/or hotline telephone service	24	11
3	Skills development (study, communications, and discussion skills)	23	10
4	Training allied professionals and/or paraprofessionals	22	10
5.5	Growth groups	17	8
5.5	Residence halls programs	17	8
7	Vocational and career development	15	7
8	Instructional related, innovation and improvement of instruction and involvement with faculty	12	5
9.5	Drugs	8	4
9.5	Orientation programs	8	4
12	Minority student programs	7	3
12	Couples and marriage programs	7	3
12	Anxiety management	7	3
14.5	Women's programs	5	2
14.5	Peer counseling	5	2
16	Sex	4	2
17	Paraprofessional programs	2	1
18	Miscellaneous programs not classified above	13	6

counselor effectiveness through programs aimed at the groups and institutions that affect individuals in order to prevent the development of problems in individuals. Counselors also need to increase their potential impact by training paraprofessionals and consulting with campus personnel who are in a position to provide services to students.

TABLE 5
Summary of Program Need Determination

How Need Determined	Number of Programs	Percent of Total
Perceived needs or interests of counseling director or staff member	106	48
Student requests	40	18
Other	26	12
School administration	19	9
Faculty requests	12	5
Formal assessment of needs—research, etc.	9	4
Informal assessment—discussion, observation, etc.	8	4

The process of establishing priorities and determining need is important in maximizing the utilization of available staff. Too often programs are based on the interests and particular skills of counselors rather than on a systematic assessment of need and establishment of goals. Only a small portion of the programs reported earlier were developed as a result of specific assessment of institutional and student needs. Once priority needs are established, specific objectives of programs can be stated so that the effects of programs can be determined. Seventy-five percent of the 220 programs surveyed reported that there was no effort to measure the effects of the programs. It seems essential that the effects of programs be determined if counselors are to meet program objectives and meet professional responsibilities.

The increasing mental health needs on the college campus coupled with limited fiscal and staff resources create the need for professionals to maximize their potential effects. Outreach programs provide one means for doing this through programs which have the potential for affecting many individuals, preventing problems from occurring, and promoting maximal development in individuals.

References

Bloom, B. L. A university freshman preventive intervention program: Report of a pilot project. *Journal of Consulting and Clinical Psychology,* 1971, *37*(2), 235–242.

Danskin, D. E. My focus for a university counseling center. *Journal of College Student Personnel,* 1965 *6*(5), 263–267.

Levy, E. I. Case study: New directions for the college counselor at CCNY. *Personnel and Guidance Journal,* 1969, *47,* 800–805.

Morrill, W. H., & Hurst, J. C. A preventative and developmental role for the college counselor. *Counseling Psychologist,* 1971, *2*(4), 90–95.

Morrill, W. H., Ivey, A. E., & Oetting, E. R. The college counseling center: A center for student development. In J. C. Heston & H. B. Frick (Eds.), *Counseling for the Liberal Arts Campus.* Yellow Springs, Ohio: Antioch Press, 1968.

Morrill, W. H., & Oetting, E. R. Outreach programs in college counseling. *Journal of College Student Personnel,* 1970, *11*(1), 50–53.

Morrill, W. H., Oetting, E. R., & Hurst, J. C. Dimensions of counseling intervention. Technical Report Number 1, 1972, Colorado State University, Grant No. R01 MH18007, National Institute of Mental Health.

11. Intervention with Married College Students

MARV MOORE
JOHN E. HINKLE
CARL CLARKE

This paper describes a new mental health approach being implemented with married students. The approach derives from a preventive mental health model and has yielded several marriage training workshops aimed at enriching the relationships of normal student couples. Three such workshops, all of which have been developed by one or more of the authors, are described in some detail. The programs represent an initial effort to create an integrated series of marriage training experiences for student couples.

PREVENTIVE MENTAL HEALTH FOR MARRIED STUDENTS

A healthy, growing marriage, satisfying and exciting to both partners, is no mere accident. It is the result of both partners obtaining a functional level of performance in the developmental tasks of marriage. There are several such tasks which are basic to the continued existence of the marriage relationship. These basic tasks include the

219

acquisition of at least the following: basic interpersonal communication skills, capacity for sustained intimacy (sexual and nonsexual), constructive management of angry feelings and actions, the ability to play and relax—the mutual experiencing of the joy of living, emotional and work separateness from one's spouse, a shared philosophy of life, and cooperative problem-solving strategies. The facility with which married partners perform these basic tasks usually increases with age, providing partners work to make it so. Furthermore, learning these basic tasks increases the probability of mastering the additional developmental tasks specific to a particular stage in the marriage process. Additional developmental tasks consist of family planning, parenting offspring through each era of child development, reorienting marriage goals after the departure of grown children, planning for retirement, and maintaining personal integrity during the final years of life. A healthy marriage is an unfolding series of growth experiences facilitated by the couple's willingness to learn new interpersonal skills and improve already acquired skills as each new stage emerges.

It is a sobering paradox to find so few educative experiences available that teach the developmental skills needed for marriage—the institution that claims most of us for the majority of our years. The premarital education received from high school and college marriage courses and from competent clergy and physicians is not adequate to prepare normal couples for the developmental tasks of marriage, let alone those persons who begin marriage with various personality deficits. And it should be noted that few couples avail themselves of these inadequate preparations for marriage.

A more optimistic outlook to this situation is emerging as developmental and preventive programs are being implemented, in marked contrast to the traditional mental health focus on dysfunction in human relationships. The "Human Potential Movement" (Howard, 1970) has spawned an array of workshop and group experiences whose main purpose is enhancing and teaching interpersonal competence. Free from physical wants and possessing more leisure, a majority of Americans actually have time and energy to think about, to practice, and to learn how to be better husbands and wives, parents, and friends. The value of achieving excellence in technological pursuits is now being applied to improving the quality of human relationships. This optimistic trend is evident in the most recent mental health literature being written for lay persons and professionals alike. One such book, *The Art of Growing,* by Robert Nixon (1962), merits further discussion because it expresses the very core of the authors' preventive mental health philosophy for married students.

Nixon posits a three-step process of discovery, experimentation, and mastery that everyone completes in gaining competence in the developmental tasks of living. Discovery is securing the affective and cognitive understanding of the historical assumptions for one's behavior. It is understanding how one has internalized the values of his culture, his parents, his peers, and significant others as they affect present feelings, fantasies, and interactions. Anxiety often accompanies the discovery process: in fact, Nixon sees anxiety as the single most important clue that a personal discovery is about to be made. Discovering one's previously unknown sources of behavior leads the growing individual to make a decision about himself. He may say: "I like the way I find myself," but more often he chooses to experiment with becoming something that he hasn't been before. By choosing to experiment he expands the possibilities of his human effectiveness and creative potential. Anxiety likewise accompanies the experimentation, since being different than one has previously acted occurs without control of the outcomes and consequences. After a while the "grower" learns what consequences follow his new actions and he then makes a choice as to whether to keep the new behavior as part of his unique repertoire of responses. When he makes this choice and when the performance of the new behavior is satisfying to the individual, he is said to have mastered the developmental task in question. Nixon's "grower" is an active, choosing, anxiety-seeking individual, always becoming what his potential will allow.

With Nixon's three-stage model of growth in mind, let us look again at the existing educative experiences for marriage in our culture. First, consider the premarital counseling offered by physicians and clergy. It is the authors' contention that all these experiences place the learner in an essentially passive role as far as discovering, experimenting, and mastering the developmental tasks of marriage. Typically the participant learns about what is good marriage, possibly some ideas about how to acquire the goodness, and maybe some minimal assessment of his or her potential to be happily married. These experiences may help the potential spouse become more active in the discovery step of growing, but only rarely is there a chance to practice the skills embodied in each developmental task. Second, consider the marriage counselor and other mental health professionals. The most competent of marriage counselors certainly attempt to help their clients become "growers" in Nixon's sense, but unfortunately their first contact with clients often occurs in times of crisis when teaching such skills may be more difficult, if not too late.

Clearly, what is needed are educative experiences which focus on the total growing process involved in accomplishing the developmental tasks of marriage. We must provide premarital and marital training experiences that assist couples in *discovering* the strengths and deficits in their relationship, that teach alternatives for *experimenting* with the developmental skills which are lacking or yet to be learned, and that afford an arena where the skills may be actively *mastered.* Furthermore, such training experiences must be made available to couples at all stages of the marital and premarital process, at a cost to participants that does not exclude any segment of the community. This paper describes several such marriage training programs which are being implemented and evaluated with college student couples.

THE STUDENT COUPLES' SEMINAR

The first marriage training experience, the Student Couples' Seminar, was developed by John Hinkle and Marv Moore (1971) at Colorado State University. The seven-session workshop has been offered to over 200 student couples during the past two years. Co-leaders for this workshop have been trained from a wide range of helping professionals and paraprofessionals. Because marriage is conceived as a process beginning with the courtship period, engaged couples are also invited to participate. The overall goal of the Student Couples' Seminar is to teach basic skills necessary for the attainment of several developmental tasks in the marriage process.

During the first session the content and philosophy for the entire seminar are first presented. A verbal commitment from participants for attending all seven sessions is obtained, and several "getting acquainted" exercises are employed. Establishing behavioral goals for each participant comprises most of the first session. Behavior goal-setting is an exercise requiring each individual participant to be very, very specific about what he wishes to accomplish as a result of the training experience.

Sessions two and three provide didactic instruction and exercises in effective communication. Five dimensions of a helping relationship (Carkhuff, 1970) are taught and practiced. The helping dimensions discussed (empathetic understanding, respect for the partner, concreteness of response, immediacy of response, and constructive confrontation) are subsequently integrated into a two-step model of communication feedback. The feedback model is an exercise where one partner begins by sending a message to the other. The second partner responds with

"What I hear you saying to me is . . ." and "That makes me feel _____ toward you right now."

Session four has three objectives: (1) increasing participants' awareness of their own physical senses and internal body states, (2) helping participants differentiate between sexual touching and caring, and affectionate touching, and (3) encouraging more caring, affectionate touching in the participants' love relationships. Achieving these objectives is accomplished by teaching deep muscle relaxation, practicing self- and other awareness exercises *a la* Gunther (1968), and by learning and practicing the rudiments of body massage.

Session five, entitled "Developing Affectional and Sexual Intimacy," affords two training exercises. First, couples isolate themselves from the rest of the group and partners mutually share memories of instances they felt especially intimate with each other. The second training experience is a group discussion exposing inaccurate cultural myths about sexuality, as well as a sharing of ideas regarding male-female differences in the sex act.

Sessions six and seven deal with constructive marital fighting. A series of nonverbal aggression exercises is practiced with the aim of increasing participants' awareness of their angry feelings. The stage model of constructive fighting is presented by the co-leaders and discussed. Finally, each couple actually proceeds through the stages of a constructive fight and is coached by co-leaders and group members.

THE CONSTRUCTIVE FIGHTING WORKSHOP

The second marriage training experience is a 14-hour marathon workshop in Constructive Marital Fighting. The two-day workshop was developed by Carol Lutker, Jane Burka, and Marv Moore at Colorado State University (see Lutker, 1971). To date this pilot workshop has been offered to five student-couple groups. The overall goal of this workshop is to teach the special skills for constructive management of anger in the love relationship.

The first day of the two-day workshop begins with each participant setting a behavioral goal he would like to accomplish as a result of the workshop; each person's goal specifies marital fighting behaviors that he wishes to improve as a result of the workshop. Nonverbal aggression exercises are then practiced to facilitate group cohesion and sensitize participants to their own angry feelings. Next each couple records an actual marital fight on video tape. After each couple's video-taped fight has been reviewed by the whole group, a two-step process of giving effective feedback is taught and practiced. For experiential contrast each couple role-plays several ineffective styles of communication feedback. Participants terminate the first day of the workshop with explicit instructions to relax, to enjoy their partners for the evening, and to engage in no fighting whatsoever until the next day.

Participants commence the second day of the fight-training experience by reviewing the behavior goals set the first day. Initial goals are further specified and discussed. Next, participants practice role-playing their partner's fighting style as observed in the video-taped fights the previous day. A stage model of constructive marital fighting (Bach, 1967) is subsequently taught and practiced with more actual fighting. In this exercise, as well as throughout the two-day workshop, co-leaders and group members give feedback to the "assailants" regarding their performance of the concepts being taught. The stage model of constructive fighting consists of making appointments for marital fights when both partners are ready to listen, fighting in rounds interspersed with think periods, and agreeing not to hit one's partner below the belt. The workshop concludes with each participant making a personalized contract with his partner and the group to practice specific behaviors that will improve his marital fighting. One month after the workshop all group members meet to discuss their performance on the goals stated in their contracts, to video tape and receive feedback on another actual fight, and to take post-workshop evaluation measures.

THE MARITAL ENRICHMENT GROUP

The third marriage training experience, the Marital Enrichment Group, was developed by Carl Clarke (1970) at the University of Florida. Over two hundred student couples have participated in this six-session (two hours weekly) marital enrichment experience. More than fifty nonstudent groups have attended a weekend marathon version of the workshop. Each Marital Enrichment Group is designed for five or six couples and provides a series of verbal communication exercises which stress the positive feelings and experiences between the marital partners. The exercises were developed on the assumptions that positive reinforcement has the strongest reward value and that a love relationship is the one which can maximally benefit from the giving and receiving of positive feedback.

Student married couples are invited to inquire about the Marital Enrichment Group through announcements in the campus newspaper and on bulletin boards. During their telephone inquiry potential participants are informed about the goals and procedures of the six-session workshop and counseled against participating if they are seeking therapy for a problem marriage. They are also invited to an orientation meeting which consists of "getting acquainted exercises" and an expanded explanation of the marital enrichment workshop.

Listed below are the topic areas of focus for each session of the Marital Enrichment Group. The interaction emphasis during each session is almost entirely upon the two married partners as a couple and upon how they are loving to each other in the uniqueness of their own relationship.

Session One

1. "Something about my partner I particularly value."
2. "Ways I want to grow, I want my partner to grow, and our marriage relationship to grow as a result of participation in this MEG."

Session Two

1. "My partner's day-to-day behavior in response to which I feel loved, respected, appreciated, valued, and understood."

Session Three

1. "My day-to-day behavior in which I am saying to my partner I love, appreciate, value, respect, and understand you."
2. "My wished-for behavior, what I wish my partner would start doing and stop doing."

Session Four

1. "The traits, qualities, habits, and characteristics that I value, respect, and admire in my partner as a person, a marriage partner, and a parent."

Session Five

1. "My needs which my partner gratifies and his (her) specific behavior which meets these needs."

Session Six

1. "Ways I and my love relationship have benefited from participation in the MEG."
2. "Loving behavior I am willing to commit myself to start doing."
3. "Loving behavior I wish my partner to commit him (her) self to doing."

Prior to each session, participants make out a behavior inventory of themselves or of their partners in the area to be discussed. Also, for most exercises, partners additionally prepare themselves for their time of sharing together by first sharing their positive feedback list with one other person or with the other husbands or wives. Sessions one, three, five, and six also begin with some awareness and nonverbal communication exercises which partners participate in together.

The "sharing seats" exercise or some modification of it is the primary method used from session to session to facilitate communication of positive feedback between married partners and the verbal expression of the "here and now" feelings experienced while listening to the positive feedback. The "sharing seats" exercise consists of one participant giving positive feedback to his (her) partner followed by the receiving partner reporting the feeling he (she) experienced while listening to the positive feedback.

By following the manual, group leaders are facilitators of verbal communication, interpersonal sharing, and small group process rather than teachers of effective skills in marriage. Essentially, each marriage partner and married pair are alternately teacher or learner as they share from their own marital experience and listen to the sharing of other couples.

Finally, it is repeatedly observed by couples who go through the Marital Enrichment Program that while the focus of the exercises is on those aspects of the marriage which are valued and appreciated, nevertheless, there is a corresponding increase in the couples' willingness to admit and discuss their problem areas and in the couples' ability to resolve their problems.

A FINAL WORD

All the marriage training programs described in this paper are action-oriented and preventive in philosophy.

They are systematic attempts to teach student couples the skills necessary for accomplishing the normal developmental tasks in the marriage process. As such, these workshops are not intended for couples who would usually seek marriage counseling or therapy, but for spouses who desire to enrich their marital relationship. A unique aspect of all these programs is the fact that each provides an arena for actual practice with evaluative feedback of the skills being taught. Experimental evaluation of each program is either being currently conducted or planned; further information may be secured by writing the authors.

REFERENCES

Bach, G., and Weyden, P. *The intimate enemy: How to fight fair in love and marriage.* New York: Wm. Morrow and Company, Inc., 1967.

Carkhuff, R. *Helping and human relations: A primer for lay professionals, volume I, selection and training.* New York: Holt, Rinehart and Winston, 1969.

Clarke, C. Group procedures for increasing positive feedback between married partners. *The Family Coordinator,* 1970, *19,* 324–328.

Gunther, B. *Sense relaxation: Below your mind.* New York: Macmillan Company, 1968.

Hinkle, J., and Moore, M. A student couples program. *The Family Coordinator,* 1971, *2,* 153–158.

Howard, J. *Please touch: A guided tour of the human potential movement.* New York: McGraw-Hill, 1970.

Lutker, C. Constructive fighting marathon for couples. Master's Thesis, Colorado State University, 1971.

Nixon, R. *The art of growing.* New York: Random House, 1962.

12. Development of a Campus Telephone Counseling Service

PATRICK E. COOK
JOHN KALAFAT
MARY TYLER

This article traces the development of a 24-hour telephone counseling service in a campus community. While the primary prevention philosophy underlying this service is not new, tracing its development highlights a number of issues that are likely to confront mental health workers who attempt to develop similar mental health services in campus communities.

The principles discussed here illustrate the community mental health principle of "mileage." The principle of mileage should be a cardinal principle in community mental health practice. Simply stated, it is this: If you are going to do something, do it in a way that has the widest possible impact. The experiences also verify the importance of including key individuals in the planning of community services.

The authors wish to thank Charles D. Spielberger and Harold A. Korn for their comments on an earlier draft of this article. Dr. Spielberger was Acting Director of the Counseling Center and Director of the Doctoral Program in Clinical Psychology at the time the original proposal was written. The Telephone Counseling Service was initiated after Dr. Korn became Director of the Counseling Center.

231

RATIONALE

Work in the areas of personal crisis and crisis intervention (Caplan & Grunebaum, 1967; Parad, 1965) indicates that many people experience periods when their usual ways of coping with life situations do not work and their patterns of living are disrupted. Because of the stresses of late adolescence and the competitive demands of most educational programs, the college years represent a period of high risk of personal crises. Consequently, enlightened university administrators take seriously their responsibility for helping students to deal with a host of factors that tend to disrupt the educational process. The stresses of college life may contribute to the development of lifelong problems if not given attention at the appropriate time.

The central notion in crisis intervention is that appropriate help, *at the time of the crisis,* can minimize the detrimental aspects and can, in fact, contribute to the personal growth of the individual. Universities have a number of formal and informal resources available for helping students—health centers, counseling centers, dorm counselors, chaplains, deans, faculty advisors, and individual faculty members. The problems with the utilization of student resources are two-fold. First, there is very little coordination and communication among resource persons in dealing with student crises. Coordination is important because the person to whom a student first turns when he gets in trouble often is not the one most qualified to help, and this person may not be sufficiently knowledgeable about other resources that would be appropriate. Second, the campus resources often have rigid routines: lengthy application forms, 9-5 hours, long waiting lists, etc. Human crises often occur at times and places which make the usual resources either unavailable or grossly inefficient. With these factors in mind, a university telephone counseling service was proposed in the Fall of 1968. At that time Florida State University had an enrollment of approximately 17,000 students, two-thirds of whom lived off campus. The students were served by rather traditional health and mental health campus resources: the Student Health Center; the Counseling Center, which at that time provided a rather narrow range of services; the University Human Development Clinic; dormitory counselors; and counselors for selected groups, e.g., international students.

THE PROPOSAL

At the request of the acting director of the University Counseling Center, who was also Director of the Doctoral Training Program in Clinical Psychology, the senior author, a member of the clinical psychology faculty, developed a brief proposal for a "university crisis service." In addition to a rationale for this service, the proposal attempted to outline its implementation and operation. In essence, a 24-hour telephone counseling service (TCS) was proposed that would make it possible for any person in the university community to talk to trained persons at any hour. It was pointed out that people often experience depression and other crisis reactions late at night or on weekends; thus, the availability of assistance at such times would be an extremely important, innovative aspect of the proposed service. Additionally, it was noted that many problems require only information or minimal supportive reassurance. For such problems, a phone call might be sufficient to enable the person to deal effectively with his present difficulty, or to "cool off" so that regular resources could then be used, i.e., a referral could be made. For more severe problems requiring specialized assistance, the phone call could provide the "first line of contact" for a referral of the telephone client to an appropriate resource where he could be seen in a face-to-face situation.

Arrangements were to be made for senior clinicians to be "on call" for consultation with the telephone counselors. Appropriate community or campus agencies that might accept referrals were also to be contacted. The referral function of the TCS would thus require that it serve as a clearing house of information about available resources. The need for close coordination and cooperation with the university health center was also stressed, since it was expected that some callers might require immediate hospitalization or emergency medical treatment.

The Telephone Counseling & Referral Service (1968) at the University of Texas at Austin, which initially served as a model for our TCS, uses advanced graduate students who are paid for their services. Our proposal called for the recruitment of selected graduate students from various mental health-related fields, including psychology, counselor education, and social work. Carefully screened undergraduates would also be sought to help staff the program. Experience in suicide prevention services has demonstrated that volunteer telephone counselors can perform effectively (Heilig, Farberow, Litman, & Schneidman, 1968). The use of volunteer counselors would have the advantage of being less expensive and providing a unique training opportunity within the campus community.

The proposal pointed out a number of direct and indirect benefits to individual students and to the university. In addition to direct service, an emergency service and crisis intervention program would serve a useful training function. It would also provide an extremely valuable research function in casting a new light on the stresses inherent in college life, and thus identifying needs for preventive programs and innovations in the delivery of counseling and other services. At a time when universities tend to be seen as dehumanizing institutions, a 24-hour information and counseling service would be responsive to student needs, and hopefully, therefore, serve to reduce the impersonality of a large university.

REACTION TO THE PROPOSAL

The six-page proposal was submitted to the Acting Director of the Counseling Center for his consideration and for staff discussion. His reaction was favorable, and he decided to share the proposal with the Vice President for Student Affairs, who referred the proposal on to the Director of the Student Health Center for his reaction.

There was an immediate negative reaction from the Director of the Student Health Center. Some of the dynamics of the negative reaction became apparent when the senior author visited with the Director of the Health Center to discuss the 24-hour TCS and to explore with him how the counseling center and health center might work together on this project. The view of the health center director was that student crises were a *medical* matter and that the health center was already adequately responding to these. In fact, he felt that the proposal was an affront to the health center, particularly since the proposal had been written without consultation with them. It was emphasized that the proposal was for discussion purposes only.

It was suggested to the Health Center Director that a 24-hour telephone counseling and information service for crisis cases would facilitate referral to the health center, which serves as a resource for the total campus community. The health director responded that his nurses on night duty would be more adept at handling student crises than would telephone counselors. It became obvious that we were not using the term "crisis" in the same way and that it appeared to be threatening to the health center staff for any other campus agency to deal with crises or emergencies.

From this experience, two lessons were learned. The first might be entitled, "Be careful how you run it up the flagpole." The flagpole approach is based upon the belief that good ideas stand on their own merit and that all one has to do is "run it up the flagpole and see who salutes it."

For community work, however, this approach overlooks many of the key human factors that are so important to program development and community planning, such as have been outlined by Klein (1965, 1968). Although the original proposal was "for discussion purposes" only, the proper track had not been laid for its implementation in terms of involving key people within the university community, particularly in the Health Center.

The second lesson learned from the encounter with Health Center personnel might be entitled "When is a crisis not a crisis?—or isn't this semantic?" It sometimes happens in community work that what matters isn't what you do, but what you call it. The term "crisis," in this instance, was interpreted by a key community figure as evidence that his bailiwick was being encroached upon. It became apparent that medical personnel and community-oriented psychologists attached different connotations to the term "crisis," with a serious miscommunication resulting. On the basis of this experience, it was decided in the future to think in terms of a "24-hour telephone counseling and information service," rather than a "crisis service." Such a 24-hour telephone service would be a logical outgrowth of the Counseling Center's "counselor of the day" program, which provided walk-in counseling every week-day afternoon.

Subsequent to the meeting outlined above, there followed the exchange of a number of memoranda. Because of the controversy generated, and because a permanent director of the Counseling Center was being recruited, the proposal was put aside for a time. When the new director for the Counseling Center was recruited, he expressed an interest in developing the service. It was recognized that further attempts to initiate the service should be made at the appropriate time, and the situation seemed appropriate in the Fall of 1969. Following several campus tragedies, an informal committee was organized to consider the question of dealing with special problems on campus. This committee had no formal charge. Rather, it consisted of representatives of the campus community, some of whom had administrative responsibility for student welfare. Committee members included the Director of the Counseling Center, the Dean of Student Development, the Director of Campus Security, an attorney from the Law School, the psychiatrist from the University Health Center, and the Dean of Arts and Sciences. While the committee's area of interest was very broad, the Director of the Counseling Center brought the original proposal to the attention of the committee and invited the author of the proposal to meet with the committee as a consultant to discuss the possibility of initiating a 24-hour counseling service.

The group expressed a willingness for the counseling center to proceed to establish a telephone counseling service, and began to consider the philosophy and the practical implications of initiating the service. It had become clear that the Health Center wished to remain uninvolved. This was unfortunate because the Health Center would have been the ideal location for the service since the personnel on duty there 24 hours a day could provide resources and social contact for the phone workers. Eventually it was decided to establish the service in a room in the Counseling Center. The group had no power to authorize funds for the operation of the TCS, and it was decided that the program would be run at minimal cost as a part of the regular services of the Counseling Center.

THE STUDENT CONSULTANTS' PROPOSAL

At this point the planning for the telephone counseling service was delegated to a group of graduate students enrolled in a seminar in Community Psychology. They were given the task of drafting a proposal for the TCS which would include guidelines for recruiting telephone volunteers, screening the volunteers, training the volunteers, developing operating procedures for the service, and evaluating its effectiveness. This gave the students a chance to be involved in the development of an actual mental health program, and to grapple with some of the practical problems which must be faced in starting a new program.

The involvement of graduate students in developing the proposal was seen as an example of community mileage. The telephone counseling service had been conceived of not only as providing service, but also as generating data about the community and campus crises, serving a training function for students in mental-health related areas (Brigante, 1965), and the initiation of the service was seen as an opportunity for students to gain experience in program development.

INITIATION OF THE SERVICE

The Telephone Counseling Service was begun on an exploratory basis during the Summer of 1970, with a number of the student consultants serving as telephone volunteers. To this core were added more volunteers, primarily graduate students in the helping professions, plus a few undergraduates. The training was loosely structured and consisted of discussions of the philosophy and policies of the TCS, familiarization with referral resources, and role playing of possible telephone crises.

With the beginning of the new academic year in September, 1970, the TCS became the responsibility of two new staff psychologists (the junior authors), along with other Counseling Center staff members from the disciplines of social work and counselor education. Major areas of activity during the 1970–71 school year were the development of procedures for screening and training volunteers, increasing the service's visibility, contacts, and referral sources, and preparation for expansion into the community in the Fall of 1971. This expansion was planned to meet pressing community needs for crisis services, to facilitate cooperation with off-campus agencies, and to broaden the training function of the TCS (Kalafat & Tyler, 1973). As the service has developed, it has come to differ in three important ways from what was envisioned in the original proposal: 1) Undergraduate, rather than graduate students, have become increasingly involved with the service, and currently constitute a majority of the volunteers; 2) students take more extensive responsibility for counseling, training, and administration than we originally expected that they would be able to assume; and 3) the role of the on-call professional back-up person has proved to be minimal, simply because students are usually able to handle situations on their own.

As the TCS is presently organized, volunteers are selected on the basis of one or more screening interviews. Each volunteer undergoes an extensive training program, which typically requires about 10 hours a week for eight to twelve weeks. This course (Theory and Practice of Crisis Intervention) has been approved for undergraduate and graduate credit in three academic departments.

The didactic portion of the training program is primarily the responsibility of the professional staff of the University Counseling Center. This includes readings and lectures on crisis intervention theory and techniques, issues in community psychology, and the problems and needs of subpopulations in the community. Practical training is conducted by experienced student volunteers under staff supervision. Techniques include discussions of procedures for handling various situations, and role playing of calls. Such sessions are usually taped, played back, and discussed by the training group. Emphasis is placed not only on counseling techniques, but also on the volunteer's awareness of his own feelings and those of the caller.

A volunteer is cleared for telephone duty only after the student trainers, the faculty coordinators, and the volunteer himself agree that he is ready to assume this responsibility. Weekly staff meetings, which include all volunteers

and professional staff members, allow the students to discuss and make decisions related to current issues in the
administration of the program, community relations, policies for handling specific problem situations, or whatever
is of current concern. Volunteers also visit community
agencies to gain information for the resource file; before
making these visits they receive training in developing
relationships with community agencies.

The development of the service during the 1970–71
school year provides further examples of previously noted
community mental health principles. As the service has
developed, it has been necessary to continue to maintain
contact with a variety of agencies and personnel, and to
keep open the lines of communication with the university
administration. Administrative acceptance is necessary
for the survival of the service, but the acceptance and
trust of students in the agency as a confidential service
might be undermined if it were seen as working too
closely with the administration (Brigante, 1969). Consequently, informal discussions with university administrators have served not only to keep key individuals
informed about the development of TCS, but also to work
with them in a relationship with the necessary balance of
support and detachment. Student volunteers have participated in some of these discussions, and have demonstrated an excellent capacity for negotiating with
administrators in direct but tactful ways.

Communication with persons who are involved with
campus mental health and mental health education has
been established in several ways. For example, the director of clinical training in the Psychology Department, the
University Chaplain, and representatives of a university
neighborhood walk-in center for drug problems have
been invited to give lectures as part of the TCS training
program. These contacts have opened the way for coordinating the work of TCS with that of other agencies concerned with campus mental health. In addition, the
process of obtaining course credit for TCS training has led

to meetings with the curriculum committees of several academic departments. These discussions have helped establish a sense of cooperation with the departments in providing students with opportunities for experiential learning.

Though the staff responsible for coordinating the TCS were careful to keep in contact with a variety of individuals and agencies in the university, they made a significant mistake in failing to communicate adequately with some of their coworkers in the Counseling Center who were not involved with TCS. The issue came to a head when the professional staff involved with TCS announced their desire to make the service available to the community as well as to the campus. Other Counseling Center staff members expressed concern about the amount of time and resources expended in the service in general, but were particularly concerned about how Counseling Center staff members, whose primary responsibility was to student development, could justify the time and resources spent in providing services to the general community. It can be emphasized that simply having an adequate rationale and administrative sanction will not prevent controversy or ensure the cooperation of all appropriate individuals. In discovering who are the appropriate individuals to be contacted, care should be taken to avoid the often fallacious assumption that the colleagues with whom a mental health worker functions every day necessarily understand or approve of all of his professional activities.

Alerted by the response of the Counseling Center staff, the TCS staff has been particularly careful to lay appropriate track for expansion of the service into the community. This has involved meetings with university personnel as well as mental health workers in the community. The timing of the expansion of the service into the community has been propitious for a variety of reasons. One fortunate occurrence was the arrival of a new Vice President for Student Affairs who shared the view that the University could and should provide some types of services to the community. While the senior author is no longer directly involved in the TCS, he continues to work in the community in an effort to facilitate university/community relations.

The visits to community agencies by TCS volunteers, supervised by the Counseling Center Staff, have left favorable impressions of the TCS in the agencies they have visited. Also, the local Mental Health Clinic is in the process of developing and seeking funds for a comprehensive community mental health center, and recognizes the need, particularly if they are to attract state funding, to develop a 24-hour crisis service, as well as a clearinghouse of information concerning the pattern of available mental health services in the community. TCS professional staff members have been involved in a series of meetings with mental health personnel from such agencies as Vocational Rehabilitation, the Mental Health Clinic, Division of Youth Services, and Division of Family Services. Such contacts appear to have impressed these mental health workers with the ability of the TCS to fill the role of an information, crisis intervention, and referral service, and they seem eager to work with the service as part of the mental health network in the community. In addition, several well-publicized incidents in which emergency assistance was unavailable after hours have sensitized the entire community to the need for a 24-hour crisis service. The response to the service verifies the need for such a service. The number of calls has steadily increased from approximately 70 during September 1970 to nearly 600 during March 1972. Analysis of recent calls indicates that approximately 30% are "counseling" calls and the remainder are chiefly information and referral calls.

It appears that TCS as it is presently being developed provides an example of the previously noted principle of "mileage." TCS is providing *direct services* by offering crisis intervention counseling, and by serving as a clearinghouse for information about patterns of services available in the community. It is also proving to be a useful vehicle for *research*. For example, a stratified sample of 463 students was given a questionnaire designed to answer the questions of who uses the service and why, who doesn't and why not. Preliminary results from this study have led to plans for more extensive research in the area of usage of student mental health resources.

Another function of the TCS is that of *university-community relations*. Relationships between professional people on and off campus have been enhanced through contacts initiated by the TCS. Though promotion of the service in the community as a whole is only beginning, this phase of the program's development offers an opportunity to improve relationships between the university and townspeople by making more generally available an effective service that is needed by the community. In addition, there is evidence to suggest that the all too common image of college students as unwashed and irresponsible is being modified as community people learn of students' willingness to work long, hard hours to be of service to others.

Finally the service provides a unique *training* experience for students. Not only are students being trained in community mental health and crisis intervention, but they are also given the opportunity to take significant responsibility for the administration and maintenance of a mental health agency. The effort to involve students as responsible decision makers in every phase of the organization not only provides desirable preprofessional training experience; it also is consonant with the idea that one goal of a liberal education is to develop responsible citizens.

REFERENCES

Brigante, T. Opportunities for community mental health training within the residential college campus complex. *Community Mental Health Journal*, 1965, *1*, 55–60.

Brigante, T. R. The assessment process in campus community mental health programs. *Community Mental Health Journal*, 1969, *5*, 140–148.

Caplan, G., & Grunebaum, H. Perspectives on primary prevention: A review. *Archives of General Psychiatry*, 1967, *17*, 331–346.

Heilig, S., Farberow, N., Litman, R., & Schneidman, E. The role of nonprofessional volunteers in a suicide prevention center. *Community Mental Health Journal*, 1968, *4*, 287–295.

Kalafat, J., & Tyler, M. The community approach: Programs and implications for a campus mental health agency. *Professional Psychology*, 1973, *4*, 43–49.

Klein, D. C. The community and mental health: An attempt at a conceptual framework. *Community Mental Health Journal*, 1965, *1*, 301–308.

Klein, D. C. *Community dynamics and mental health*. New York: Wiley, 1968.

Parad, H. *Crisis intervention: Selected reading*. New York: Family Service Association, 1965.

Telephone Counseling and Referral Service. *Annual Report*. The University of Texas at Austin, July, 1968, (Mimeo).

Part IV

EPILOGUE

13. Psychological Stress in the Campus Community

A Conversation with Joseph Katz, Seymour Halleck, and Nevitt Sanford

Editor's Note: What follows are excerpts from a two-hour conversation with three superb human beings whose own lives have been deeply and productively intertwined with those of college students. Because of limitations in permissible manuscript length, only about half of the conversation is reproduced here. Shortening the original transcript of the conversation has been a grim process, but I've tried to retain what seemed to me the most important aspects of the conversation while doing justice to the participants' own thoughts and modes of expression.

BLOOM: Our topic is psychological stress on the college campus and perhaps I can try to begin by making this observation. Anybody who's followed the status of American colleges in the last twenty years can't help but be impressed with how much they've changed and how much students have changed. And yet I think people wonder whether there is fundamentally any difference between the college students of today and the college students of twenty years ago or, to put it another way, whether in fact the stresses that operate on students are really appreciably different now from the ones that may have operated on the students in the early fifties. I wonder what impression you have about the continuity of stress over the past couple of decades. Do the stresses operating on students seem to you to be substantially different from those that existed in the past?

KATZ: That's a good question. I think there are both continuities and discontinuities. The continuities are observed in the problems of psychological development, relations with parents, relations with peers, and achieving autonomy. This continuity is there not just over decades but over centuries. Another continuity is that students in the fifties too were not satisfied with the curriculum. They too thought that it did not touch them where they lived. It did not sufficiently orient them toward occupation and further life roles. Their own curiosity was not the kind that their professors pursued or pretended to pursue when they were teaching them, and all this made for a good deal of implicit discontent. We know how the students handled this, by fleeing into their own collegiate culture, the gentleman's "C," and other ways of doing what one needed to do in order to stay in college while really not being very much affected by the values, intellectual and otherwise, that the faculty stood for. However, there was an implicit respect for authority and very much an acceptance of *in loco parentis*, which meant that students would grumble and try to evade it in many ways and get an enjoyment out of this evasion, but the basic premises were very much accepted.

In other areas the differences are rather enormous. One outstanding fact about the present generation is that they have increasingly lost much of the sense of respect for authority, whether it be teachers or other kinds of adults, and this has thrown them back more on their own resources, both in the direction of developing more independence and also more anxiety. In addition, we have the rather widespread phenomenon either of direct activism or of taking a critical stance toward society. The student response can be demonstrations, more quiet activities, such as social services, or escape from the culture by way of drugs, various forms of encounter groups, communes, or very strongly aesthetic, sensuous, or sensitive styles of living.

Also greatly different, and increasingly so, are the relations of women to men, with the women having a sense of having been in the past much suppressed. More important than even the women's looking for different roles in the occupational or social worlds, is their emotional development, their sense of autonomy, their asking the men for a different emotional response. Studies that we have done recently show that there is a marked contrast between men and women in regard to whether they are tying sex and affection together. The women are increasingly asking the men to respond to them in terms of affectionate relationships and not just in terms of sex alone. At the same time women are freer in regard to sex. This greater sexual freedom also means that crises in male-female relationships are experienced earlier; for a number of students as early as the freshman year. At the moment one gets the feeling of being in a transitional phase where the old sexual mores have been broken and new norms are beginning to develop. There is an increased anxiety on the part of both males and females, and so here is another area of social stress.

Finally, one can make a distinction between the last half of the sixties and the first two or three years of the seventies, and that is that in the latter part of the sixties students reacted to the stresses that they perceived in the society and in themselves with a feeling of hope that these things could be coped with. Externally, they could bring war to an end; they thought they could bring racism to an end or nearly to an end. As far as inner problems were concerned, drugs first held out a promise. The encounter groups held out a promise, and in all of these were hopes of inner liberation. At the present time we have a good deal of despair, outwardly about the possibilities of society being responsive either in the realms of politics, ecology, or the economy, and inwardly because so many attempts at remedy and solution have run their course and have not delivered. Encounter groups have not brought liberation, and drugs are rarely still seen as an instrument of psychological salvation. We have now a moment of depression, or at least a much more passive mood. Part of this I ascribe to the failure of adults to use the enthusiasm, the readiness of the young, that existed in the second part of the sixties. But the situation of adolescents and young adults in regard to society has been fundamentally redefined. They are never going to go back to accepting a subordinate role the way they did in the fifties.

BLOOM: Sy, from your exposure to the college scene over the last few years, how do you view the changes in the character of the stresses that face students?

HALLECK: For me the major stress has been what's going on in the world, and the situation in the universities just reflects trying to keep up with changes in the society, the whole issue that so many people have written about, the rapid technological change, the fact that things are not predictable, the tendency to live in the present. I think the best way I could put it is that twenty years ago there was a high probability that if you did certain things in school, certain logical and often salutory consequences would follow. That is no longer true today. I think the college student today lives with a certain sense of unpredictability and uncertainty. He often reacts to that state by doing nothing, by waiting, by becoming angry, and by becoming depressed. I think the real problem is where we are in the world, whether we can tolerate the rate of change, the whole future shock we are currently experiencing, and of course it hits the young first.

BLOOM: Nevitt, how does the college student seem to you in comparison with ten or twenty years ago? Do you think there've been some fundamental changes?

SANFORD: The thing that strikes me about this question is how little we know. When you say college students, are you talking about college students nationwide, community colleges, the whole range of colleges? I think that if you had the means to study truly representative samples of all college students in this country, you'd get a very different kind of picture than we in fact get by looking at students at Reed, Berkeley, NYU, et cetera. There's no question in my mind but that we have something new. There are certain psycho-historical types present now that are absolutely brand new, that we have never encountered before. But if you were to give some of these scales, such as MMPI or OPI, nationwide, what would stand out would be how different other students, let's say the University of the Pacific, or Central Michigan University, would be from the students that get the attention, that the journalists write about, that the concepts of the new culture are based on. If you look at Feldman and Newcomb's new book in which they put in tabular form all the studies in which the F scale has been used, or the social maturity scale, which is the F scale backwards, the distribution at Reed College about six years ago was so high on social maturity that it didn't even overlap with the University of the Pacific. So the educational task at Pacific and Central Michigan is still how to liberate students from the narrow, constricted, authoritarian way in which they face the world, in contrast to places where students have become highly sensitive to the big changes in society.

BLOOM: I don't know whether student activism is contagious or whether there are some universities that are somehow the harbinger of the future. It's an interesting problem that I've never been able to think through. Whether what happens first at Berkeley and at Columbia spreads across the country like a contagion, or whether Reed College is simply the College of the Pacific ten years from now. That is, is there some inevitable transition that takes place in young people, and because each university may attract a different kind of student, the pacing of that transition is different, and where the students are along that history may be different?

SANFORD: I think we've all made some observations that would support that. I mean, I've been to places in the late sixties where people were saying that what happened in Berkeley and at Stanford three or four years earlier was really hitting them now. But, of course, the whole picture has changed now. That trend of contagion has kind of broken up.

KATZ: Contagion isn't really quite the right word, not only because of its disease implications, but also because what happened was not so much that somebody started it and somebody else imitated it, but rather that conditions in all these places were fairly similar and students often had parallel reactions that preceded knowledge of what others were doing. I also want to challenge that it began at Berkeley, because it also began with the Black students in the South sitting at the lunch counters.

BLOOM: You're not impressed that that is an imitative phenomenon?

KATZ: No, but there are some people who first discover certain modes of social expression. It might happen at one place first in this or that respect, but the underlying conditions are similar. It is also in part a class phenomenon. We know from the studies of the white activists that they tend to come from more affluent backgrounds, have experienced some kind of leisure, less anxiety about their place in society, and hence, have more psychological energy available to think about society at large. People who belong to classes of lower status have often been more oriented towards making it into the middle class.

HALLECK: There is a current position that as more and more upper middle class kids of white, Anglo-Saxon, Protestant, or Jewish background who used to go into the professional positions are dropping out of the system, there is more room for the ethnics and Southern Baptist, lower class types, who are moving into college seriously, into community colleges and other places, who are behaving just as the so-called elite behaved in the 50's, and are gradually going to accumulate power and the position that other groups have.

SANFORD: We found out last year that the bankers and industrialists in the Bay Area are not worried about their ability to attract suitable employees. They just wouldn't get as many Stanford types who want to go into business. There's a considerable dropout of middle class youngsters who were heading for jobs in the most established sectors, but they weren't worried because there were plenty of students from the University of the Pacific who were going up in the world, and the jobs being vacated by the turned-off middle class kids would happily be taken over by them.

HALLECK: I think one thing the radicals kept forgetting is how big this country has gotten. With all the protest about the draft there were still enough people to be drafted, and with all the people dropping out of the system there were still enough young people in other areas to move into the system.

SANFORD: That's right, and there is another remark that should be made here. Namely, that if we're going to make generalizations about college students and about the differences between college students of today and the fifties, we have to consider as enormously important the types of students who were not in college in the fifties, and I not only need to mention the ethnic minorities, but also the community college people.

BLOOM: Do you two tend to agree with Joe that some of the stress that preoccupies college students has had a very stable quality over the years, that the whole set of developmental tasks that kids are into today is really not appreciably different from what was the case fiteen or twenty years ago?

HALLECK: Ten years ago I would have said that the commonest causes of emotional difficulty were dissolution of a close relationship with a boy or girl and failing in school, and I think that's still true.

SANFORD: I think that's still true. If we are talking about developmental tasks, as Joe was mentioning in the beginning, like the two that Sy mentioned also, relations with one's family and getting a job, I mean these things are still there, but over the long haul we probably are getting some changes. For example, authoritarianism in college students. In fact, authoritarianism itself, as it was described in the late forties, is probably a different phenomenon today than it was then. There's something almost quaint and anachronistic about the kind of authoritarianism that was described in the 1940's. It is not only that ideology has changed but family life is changing. You can't very well expect that we will continue to get the same sort of ways of dealing with authority when the role of the father in the family has been changing so rapidly. The whole family structure is changing rapidly in the direction of fewer children and totally different patterns of family life as more and more women work, have fewer and fewer children, and this old father presiding over this submissive wife and little flock of kids, this image is really bound to be changing, in which case we can't possibly get the same sorts of personality types that we did. Another thing I wanted to mention that I think has changed over the long haul is the more rapid maturation. I guess we also get more rapid physiological maturation than we used to, but kids are being introduced to more and more experiences of life earlier and earlier. Often by the time you get a middle class kid into college, he has already had most of the great experiences that we had in college, even in graduate school, and he's already jaded. You wonder what in the world could possibly excite this young person other than louder and louder noises or more and more stimulating kinds of things. This is a real change in our culture and I think it has to do with today's communications explosion. Everybody is onto something right away partly because of the media. Everything comes crowding in on the youngsters, and the experiences are happening earlier and earlier. I think that's rather sad in the sense that we're getting into a state of affairs in which behavior is less meaningful, so to speak. A sexual relationship on the part of a fourteen-year-old kid couldn't possibly have the same meaning as if this occurred for the first time when he was eighteen, let's say, because there's less *to* him at that time. There's less there in the person that can connect with this experience and thereby make the experience more meaningful, and you find young people who actually are after the behavior, and evaluate each other in terms of their behavior. One type of young person that we see in our little clinic is the young woman who's been into sex already for quite awhile in high school, but she feels inferior because she's really not had an orgasm or not good orgasms, and furthermore, it appears that she is incapable of relationships with men. It's sexual politics, you might say. She uses men in order to fix her self-conception with respect to sexual behavior. The idea that a man might be a friend or someone to relate to on another basis hasn't yet occurred to her.

KATZ: It is true that sexual experience has occurred earlier. In our studies, the first occurrence is more likely at age 16 or 17 than age 14. I had thought earlier that integration of sex in the personality required a certain amount of delay, and hence, that if it did come later it would be more mature. I'm beginning to question that notion because what went with the delay was a good deal of mystification about sex that prevented facing up to some of the problems of relationships; there was that sense of some kind of magical solution once one established the sexual relationship. It is true that problems of impotence or failure to achieve orgasm are now reported for much younger people. But how many women in their thirties or forties have not yet come to grips with the problem of impotence in their partners or with their own sexual difficulties? So even though the present situation causes the young more anxiety, I wonder whether the demystification of sex may not also be a factor leading to a greater maturing of relationships.

HALLECK: There's one paradox in the sexual revolution which continues to confront me, and I see it causing a lot of emotional difficulties. If you want a relationship where you can get as close as you can to another individual, it requires some hope of permanency or at least longevity, and the paradox is that you try to get as close as possible to another person, but at the same time know that you're not going to stay together—I think this leads to all kinds of inauthentic behaviors and a high degree of casualties when these relationships break up. One can build a large psychiatric practice in a university community just by dealing with people who are coming out of a living-together relationship. The other issue is that male impotence is a bigger thing probably because it's always been easier for men, at least in this country, to relate to women as sexual objects. It's much easier to make love to an object if you're the least bit insecure, and as women are demanding that they be less objectified, and as there is greater knowledge that the woman can enjoy and should enjoy sex, the men are put in a spot which they're not really ready to get into.

SANFORD: I think this is to be remarked in personal relationships generally, man and man, woman and woman, as well as between the two sexes. I encounter a lot of young people who come to California, and it turns out that they've made no friends in college who are still their friends. They haven't related to anybody with the expectation that a friendship is a friendship. When you relate to somebody, this becomes virtually a part of yourself. In the old days, one of the points about going to college was that that was where you made your friends who would be your friends for life. I don't see this expectation among college students very much today, and the youngsters who come to California, they don't keep in touch with the people back East. They just find somebody in California who plays the same role in their lives, or they look for the same kind of group, the same kind of life style, and that's what is durable rather than interpersonal relationships.

HALLECK: It implies a denigration of individuality. There's an indication that people are interchangeable. Incidentally, we suffer from that too. Even if you settle permanently in one of the university towns, sooner or later most of your friends will leave you.

KATZ: I very much agree with you about fidelity in relationships and the cumulative feelings that happen between two people when there's been a long history. But the fact of married life, particularly in this country, is that there has been no permanency. I don't just mean the divorces. With many couples, even if they have been together for a long time, there really is no great permanence of relationship. I agree with you about the casualties. Any break-off is terribly hard. Divorce is a most psychologically searing experience to have. I wonder whether going through that experience quite early does not really impress on one's self the value of greater steadiness and of making a more permanent choice.

BLOOM: You seem to be saying that some of the stress that college students feel is part of their normal developmental task and, as Joe says, that some of those tasks are dealt with earlier than perhaps was the case some years ago. You're also saying that some of that stress, to the extent that it's different from what students were into a couple of decades ago, is really coming at students from the outside. The world is changing, future shock, et cetera, and that's led me to wonder whether in fact there is any kind of psychological stress that's unique to the campus, or whether you're just talking about young people, whether they happen to be high school graduates now at work, or whether they are students at a university. Do you think there is a kind of special subset of stresses that characterize the university student as separate from any young person of eighteen or nineteen years?

KATZ: The word stress has to be understood as something that can bring out potentialities in people. The experience of stress is itself a sign of growth. It means that something is being envisaged that is difficult to achieve or to which there might be obstacles. College students experience stress very differentially, and for some people it is hardly experienced at all. Some students continue the dependency patterns that they acquired in the home and continue them into later adult life; they transfer from dependency upon parents to dependency upon spouse. But the college situation provides opportunities that people who do not go to college do not have. One of the opportunities is the presence of teachers, not enough of them, who represent attitudes, knowledge, and life styles different from those encountered in the parental culture. Also the peers are different. There is also the opportunity for a moratorium because there is no immediate need for commitment occupationally, socially, maritally; that again provides an opportunity for letting things come to the surface that might be foreshortened in other people. One might say that there are more opportunities of stress for college students and absences of developmental stress for the noncollege-going.

SANFORD: I would say that the college students are the lucky ones at that age, if you consider the situation of an eighteen- or nineteen-year-old working on the line at General Motors. I've known college kids who have had summer jobs in these plants, and they were really appalled by getting some knowledge of the lives of the young people next to them who weren't going any place other than some sort of job like this.

HALLECK: There is another difference. The kid who is not in school, more than the kid who is in school, lives in a three-generational community, whereas I think the student lives in a one-generation community for the most part. The working young man or woman is generally more likely to have access to older people and children.

KATZ: The college situation provides an opportunity for experiencing stresses before a commitment is made to a life style that might foreshorten certain developmental possiblities. This stress is productive of growth because it may mean a new perception, a confrontation, a crisis, an opportunity for striking out in a different direction, a different way of feeling, a different political attitude, a different way of relating to other people. This is not so much provided in the situation of the noncollege-going young person. Two other things can be said about the noncollege-going person. One is that even if you take into account the depression and the loneliness of the college student, there is an even more immobilizing depression and apathy of the noncollege youth that student interviewees who have worked have reported to us. This depression comes from a restricted occupational and life space. They cannot go very far because so much is closed to them. There also is what one might call the Studs Lonigan phenomenon, that is, a very direct kind of sensuous, even motoric expression that is not adequately brought under control, so there might be getting drunk, explosive violence that brings abortive contact with the cognitive, intellectual, aesthetic possibilities in the person.

SANFORD: But don't you think that the thing about a college education, if it works at all, is that you practically have to have something of the likes of college in order to be sensitive to the future shock thing? Being into politics seriously really requires a certain stage of moral development, you might say, so that the person is capable of some sense of identification with larger aggregates of people, so that he worries about this kind of thing. Which means that he can get into kinds of moral conflicts that would be totally foreign to a person who hadn't reached the place where the world was defined in such fashion for him. I'm not saying that this young nineteen-year-old man working for General Motors is not political, but, of course, the great complaint about labor unions is that politics for them is bread-and-butter and working conditions, and we don't any longer expect them to take any enlightened or progressive views with respect to larger political issues. That will have to be the task of the educated people.

BLOOM: Well, I want to push that one step further. We are all sitting here, deeply identified with the university and with the problems of university life and with the problems of college students. I've written someplace that America's college students are our greatest national treasure and yet the fact is that the college student of today is very much on the defensive compared to how he was a decade or two ago. In fact, the university is on the defensive. It's being attacked from the left, it's being attacked from the right, and what you revere so much in the college student as the leader of the future, and the way he brings his thought processes to bear on larger problems, isn't revered generally in this country. It seems to me there's been quite a reduction in the status attributed to universities, certainly to professors, and, I believe, in large measure to students as well.

SANFORD: That makes me think of what is really the greatest strain on the intelligent and sensitive college students, and that is the betrayal of them by the university. They had great expectations of the university. They thought they would find their moral leadership as well as intellectual leadership and instead they find a kind of jungle of extreme corruption. Most universities are dominated by people who will do anything to get money and the students know that. They know that their leadership, the people that they're supposed to respect, are not really exerting any leadership. They are playing politics to keep this thing going, never mind what its reasons for existing might be, and as the university has become more and more an instrument of national policy, more and more dependent on government support, this has become even clearer to the students. So, in a way they have no place to go. They have no models of adult responsibility. They look at their professors. They see them not as men who are dedicated to higher values but who are dedicated to getting more status and power for their specialty or for their department and most of their professors are completely cynical, and the students also know that. The professors have long since abandoned any hope of the great achievements that could be imagined and are just "carrying on." They've made their adaptation with the facts of life in the university and they have found a comfortable way to live, and that's about it.

HALLECK: To get into the university community either as professor or student presents you with a kind of sensitivity to how bad things really are. It's much easier in some ways to be a lower class kid who works in a factory because you can adopt simplistic answers to problems. Whereas, once you get into school you start realizing how complicated things are and how difficult solutions are, and you're more or less overwhelmed with the burden.

SANFORD: It's a temptation to cop-out, as they say, or to find some restricted life style that really doesn't involve oneself in these big issues.

HALLECK: I'd agree that we professors certainly haven't solved the problem for ourselves, and I don't think we've provided an adequate model.

SANFORD: What I said was a very strong statement. Obviously there are other kinds of professors around, but they are rarer than they used to be. I think students can count themselves lucky if they find one in the course of their growing-up.

HALLECK: How much of the professor's withdrawal has been heightened by the radical movement? One of the things I sense on campuses is the tendency for professors to become more cynical, become more involved in their own careers. It seems, if anything, to have been heightened by the fears they have of student militancy.

KATZ: Another related source of stress is that the university is not really a community and, most importantly, that the professors are not a service class. They are defined officially and rhetorically as teachers, which means rendering a service to students. But as we all know, professors rarely receive training for teaching and rarely receive in-service training. Teachers spend little time thinking about the task of pedagogy. What we have is a class of people, the professoriate, which has one kind of interest, the pursuit of specialty and the pursuit of promotion and status, and we have the students, who are looking to this group for service that's not coming. I think this pulling in different directions is another very important source of stress. Another is that what a student does in college is not sufficiently related to what he will do when he leaves, not just in his occupation, but in his life style. We can call this anticipatory stress.

BLOOM: Well, a lot of what you're saying is in a sense an indictment of higher education. That is, you're laying some proportion of the problem at the feet of higher education. The university is under attack; either it costs too much, or it is elitist, or it's irresponsible, or it's self-serving. Every time you indict the university about something, you say in effect that some of the attack that comes from the legislature may be quite justified. If you say that there is something corrupt about the way in which the faculty functions, if the university is a place where the faculty will do anything for money, then in a way it's hard to defend yourself against the attack that comes from the funding sources.

SANFORD: But I would say that, nonetheless, because my interest is in preserving something of the ideal of the university, that the greatest dangers to it do not come from the state legislature, they come from the lack of imagination of the people who are supposed to be running it. A good example would be psychology itself. Most of the work which psychologists do is utterly trivial, and it contributes nothing to the solution of the problems of society, which is not so bad, but psychologists insist on getting money for it, as if they did contribute something to the problems of society. It would be very civilized and very much in the tradition of the university if a psychologist said, "I'm studying this because I'm curious about it and I find this really quite fascinating," and if he could convey something of that fascination with that problem to his students. Even with your experimental psychologist today, he's getting funded by the federal government on the grounds that somehow or other this is going to build a science which in just a few years is going to be of great service to humanity, and then if they put pressure on him to apply something or other, then he takes these simplistic laboratory models and acts as if they really held for life. Education is the worst offender in this respect. The psychologists have taken little models of learning from the laboratory and tried to act as if school rooms corresponded in some fashion to this laboratory situation, which is a way of making a mockery out of learning in the schoolroom situation. We've known for years that teachers could never apply anything that they learned in educational psychology. It was totally unrelated to the problems that they encountered in the schoolroom. You can't take an abstract principle about learning, an abstract finding which exists because it has been abstracted from the context of the child himself or herself, and apply that, because in the schoolroom this occurs in real people, whom you have to deal with. So there's a vast aggregate of irrelevancy and triviality, which is okay as an expression of the peculiar curiosities of psychologists, but it's humbug to suppose that this vast psychology establishment should be supported by the nation because of its contribution to human life.

KATZ: Nevitt, does an illustration come to mind?

SANFORD: I would make reference to the kind of learning theory that has made the teaching machine possible. They've got something there. It's quite possible to show there are certain kinds of rote learning that can be taught in a mechanical way, and so then the next step is to start a business of putting together teaching machines, and then this plays right into the hands of most conservative educators who don't want to do anything except present bits of content in an orderly fashion anyway, and so the whole conception of education is degraded, and psychologists are right in there contributing their share.

HALLECK: Let me switch around what you said, Bernie, about the university being under attack. Maybe there is something very good about the attack. I for one welcome it. In the fifties and for part of the sixties, universities existed in splendid isolation from the community. They were a system that was not monitored by the people, either by the left or the right, and I think anytime you get a social system going that only is reviewed by itself, the system inevitably gets corrupt. It makes little difference whether you're talking about the government or whether you're talking about organized psychiatry as I know it. We have learned repeatedly that as long as a system is only monitored by its people, it will eventually fail to meet needs for which it started out, and sure it's tough now and we're under a lot of fire, but I have some optimism that out of all this pressure we're under we can come up with a better university system.

KATZ: Still I would say part of the attack is not the attack that we are making here, but is very much on the wrong principles. The legislature often attacks what is essential in a university, and that is its freedom of inquiry and dissent. They have often objected to those students who have been asserting themselves or pressing for better teaching and better curricula. This self-assertion has aroused the ire of the legislators, and that part to my mind is sinister. They are not necessarily helping us in the needed kind of criticism.

HALLECK: In other words they've reached the same conclusions from different motivations. I suppose one issue is tenure, for example. Most of us defend it on the grounds that it enables us to have freedom, but on the other hand, attacking tenure is not all bad because we know that universities are loaded with people who are not doing any work.

SANFORD: It's filled with irony because it's been so long since a tenured professor has ever said anything controversial. All the people who are saying the controversial things are the assistant professors, and they don't have any protection of tenure. By the time you get to be a tenured professor, you're so close to, you're so fully into, the whole thing that you're not likely to frighten the legislature or anybody else.

KATZ: I think that the people who are now not doing any work will continue in the institutions. Society's interest in institutions is less in terms of what we have been talking about and stems more from the desire for social control. One reason we have colleges and have social support for them is that they keep the kids off the streets. For a while the universities were attacked as costly, but the public is beginning to realize that colleges are cheaper than the Peace Corps or Vista or similar kinds of organizations, and cheaper than jails. For that reason we will probably be continuing, even with potshot attempts at restricting us.

BLOOM: I want to try to convert these comments into what, in your judgment, their programmatic significance is. First, we would begin with the premise that not all stress is bad. As Joe mentioned, and I think Sy too, growth comes out of stress, and so I don't think anyone is proposing that we build a university that is stress free. But given that stress is not all bad, the issue still is what can the university do to create that kind of environment, or that kind of atmosphere, for its students, and its faculty, and its staff, to work in so that the experience is of such a growth-inducing character that the alumni become friends of the university rather than its enemies. Now, I suppose one way to approach the problem is to imagine that the three of you have the opportunity to construct a brand new university, and you can work together, and share your ideas, and implement whatever you want to do. The issue is not specifically what you would do, but what the principles are that would govern what your decisions would be about how to create this new kind of community.

KATZ: You're really referring to a pipe dream of ours, and we are looking for somebody who'll give us the money to start such a college. First of all, it would be built on the contract principle, as far as learning is concerned, which would mean that a student's curiosity would be one guide in the development of the tailor-made curriculum for him, and he would determine which areas he wants to learn in conjunction with faculty, and he would be subject to evaluation criteria at the speed appropriate to him.

BLOOM: So your first point, then, is that the student would have a much more active role in determining the criteria of his educational attainment.

KATZ: Then, secondly, as far as the curriculum is concerned, he would very much more be subject to experiences which would go beyond experiences he had in his prior upbringing. They would bring him in contact with different kinds of social classes, with different ethnic groups, and would bring him in contact with people psychologically and culturally different from himself. He would be very much more actively engaged in exploration than in textbook learning alone. I would include a higher learning principle, that learning often takes place best in groups. I would have teamwork, people working on joint projects as an essential part of the curriculum. In regard to relationships with peers, there would be considerably greater attention to the facilitation of adequate relatedness, to the management and development of tender feelings and the understanding of hostile feelings. We would not think that a student will acquire his general education only while he is in college. Much more emphasis would be put upon the furtherance of his curiosity, his own independent way of furthering it, and we would assume that it is going to be very much a continuing process. I would relate college to the student's concerns about his occupational future and his future life style. The great tragedy of America is that most people work at humdrum routine jobs and live in routine environments, the many tracts of this country which are culturally and psychologically impoverished. I see the universities as the great proving grounds, the great laboratories for different kinds of life styles.

BLOOM: Sy, what about student support services in the future? This means not only services for casualties, but it means some kind of attention to preventive intervention on the campus. If you had the power to design such a support system for this new university, what are the things you'd try to keep in mind?

HALLECK: One of the things I'm thinking about as I sit here is that no future universities ought to be built in isolated areas. It just shouldn't happen. Universities should be part of communities. And I think the issue for student support services is how to create a community which is more than one-generational, and I'm very much into the idea of having a university where not only people of a certain age group are present, but where the student body includes older people as well, and includes professors and supporting staff. I think the one function of any student affairs persons is to have a job in which he tries to do himself out of a job. I don't see an enormous role for student support services. I think perhaps the amount we have now may be excessive in some ways, and if universities actually were in the community, such support services could be combined with other services within the community, and the uniqueness of the student role would not be so powerful and precious. I think both students and the community would be much better off. Earlier you asked me what would our vision be of the university if you could create one, and I have a special fantasy about that, being a futurist. I would like to see a significant portion of the curriculum devoted to future studies and general systems theory, which I think is the prime need of our civilization.

SANFORD: I would start first with the consideration of the purposes in education and the university, and insist again that the goals of undergraduate education have to be stated in individual developmental terms, which puts the accent on teaching which induces progressive developmental changes in students, rather than on simply making sure that every conceivable kind of content is to be taught. I would say the same would hold for graduate training, in that we must abandon the idea that we must teach everything that can be taught in Graduate School and turn out products who know everything already. The most we can hope to do in Graduate School, or should hope to do in Graduate School, is to teach people how to learn, or to start a process of becoming an inquiring kind of person, and the thing is that if you look at it that way, you find yourself allied with the state legislature who wonders what the professors are doing with their time. If the professors insist that education is a matter of courses, units, and credits, they invite the question, "Isn't it possible to do this in a more efficient way?" Professors keep on defining education that way, they never mention any of the other values of university life, any of the other processes which would be beneficial to students. We have this extremely ironic situation in which I say that colleges and universities are unnecessarily expensive precisely because they undertake to teach too much, and that what they undertake to teach has nothing to do with any kind of theory of what students may be like or how students develop. They do it because they are providing jobs for professors, and serving the interests of professors, who are interested in building up their specialties and expanding the body of knowledge. To me, it's clear as day that you can provide a better undergraduate education at a place like St. John's College, which is very inexpensive, because teachers teach the whole curriculum. Every teacher is there to lead students into various fields of inquiry. It is remarkably economical, and on the whole students get a much better general education. I'm not holding to the precise curriculum that they have, but the idea of an intellectual community in which teachers range over a variety of disciplines, and talk to each other, is very economical compared with our usual thing of making sure that we've got somebody who can teach medieval French or whatever. So that if you can let loose from the idea that this total content of knowledge must somehow be taught, or else you don't rate as a university, then the way is wide open for all kinds of innovations.

KATZ: I think Nevitt put his finger on one of the fundamental problems, and that is the course/credit/unit system, which has produced a conception of teaching as an impersonal act that could just as well be done by a machine, by a screen, or any other kind of device, and often is, even if you have a living professor in front of you. But I'm very much struck by the difference between the psychiatric model of education and the academic model of education. The psychiatrist takes a long time with one patient, expecting very little progress, because he knows how resistant the psychological processes are, how long it takes to learn something. As a colleague of mine remarked facetiously, "Any year something is going to happen in this psychoanalysis." We know from studies that learning cannot take place adequately unless there is an older person who is encouraging, who is stimulating, who is supportive, and who is available. This ingredient is largely missing for most students in our colleges and universities. Far from having too many teachers, as some legislators think, we have too few.

One way to deal with this is to enlist students as teachers of each other under the tutelage of the faculty. Another resource is what I call the extramural faculty, the people in the community who are able to teach, who have experiences and skills often considerably different from those of present faculty. Law schools and medical schools already use such people as the so-called clinical or adjunct faculty. We can also use many of the very capable adults in our universities, who are now unused: the counseling service, the health service people, the administrative people. Take the health service. The way it still operates in almost all institutions is that you come in, you get a pill, or you get an examination. You are an object. There is no educational gain from this interaction. In fact, there is an educational deficit, because you're slightly more alienated from your body which the doctor can manipulate like a machine. I see the possibility of using the doctors, when the patient comes in with an illness, to provide an opportunity for instruction about how the student's body functions. This is one instance of how the service function could become part of the teaching function. Another thing I'd like to mention as part of my ideal university is not just student development, but also faculty development. It means that the faculty also become learners. They'd be as much engaged in the process of learning new things as the students are. Further, one of the social pathologies of the faculty is that they have never left school. We need to provide more opportunities for faculty to live and work in other environments than that of school, precisely because they can bring back to their students, and to themselves, these other kinds of life experiences.

HALLECK: I think where things are going, if universities become truly community universities, then adjunctive services, such as student health, for example, will have no relevance on their own as separate detached units. I think student health will disappear very quickly once national health insurance is a fact in this country, because there will be no reason at that point to treat students separately. What you will need is a medical service available in the community that treats students as well as other people. Of course, as long as there are outlying universities, there will have to be special health services, but I think that's an anachronism.

KATZ: But this depends on whether a National Health Service is just going to dispense services for more people. In that case, there will still be good reason to have a separate kind of health service, if it could do some of the educational tasks, and not just the fixing of a hernia and the prescribing of a pill.

BLOOM: Joe sounds like he's not very optimistic that the National Health Insurance program is going to change the ideology of American medicine. It's going to change the way they get paid, but not their ideology.

HALLECK: Well, let me say, as a doctor, that it's a very elitist use of resources to put as many doctors as we do in universities.

KATZ: But it wouldn't be elitist if the purpose of it were to train students in the better understanding of themselves. Then these students would themselves become agents in their community to convey that kind of knowledge. Part of the orientation would be a public health care delivery orientation. It would make physician assistants of our students. This leads me to say that community orientation of what is learned in college is now almost nonexistent. My ideal college would make this very much a part of the education of the student, orienting him to what he can do with his knowledge, making it useful to others.

SANFORD: What you were saying earlier about these new patterns of teaching, the new kinds of teachers, and so on, all that depends on a different view of what education is. You have to define education in terms of more general qualities that you are trying to develop in students before you can talk seriously of getting rid of this tremendous academic apparatus that is holding us back. Concerning the student health services, or student development in general, I would say that we have to have a conception of human development and knowledge of human development, about how people actually develop, and then we must design communities in order to develop people. If you do that, the gap between what we do on the student services and what we do in the classroom begins to disappear.

BLOOM: You're talking about physician in the original use of the term, that is, physician as teacher.

SANFORD: That's what the Wright Institute is about, and we probably will become a university. It's very hard to prevent us from moving that way too fast, actually. The big push is to have a graduate training program in futurology or system theory. We'll teach psychology. We'll teach about individuals, but mainly we will teach about the systems that are now present and will develop in the future, and we have to have some people who know about that but who don't lose sight of individual processes. So our next development in graduate education will probably be in the direction of a more generalist, systems-oriented, futurology type of psychological social science, and the way is wide open for this. We've got the student applicants; we've got the professors. All we need is someone who will commit himself to organizing the program. The same is true of undergraduate education. Our place would actually be a better school if we had undergraduates around so that our graduate students would have more teaching to perform. They do teach each other. We have graduate students who give more or less formal seminars about something that they are expert in before they ever became graduate students. They can teach this material to newcomers or to those who would like to look into this, and they do. That's a nice economy that you can make. After all, people used to define the university as a company of people who want to teach each other. I think it's fair to say that a number of these principles are already in our graduate school, and you see, this school is run by students, in the sense that they have a major voice in what's going to be done with their money. It's the only school I know of for which that's true, and wait until state legislatures hear about this, or wait until the conservative economists hear about this, that if you've got something that people want, they'll pay for it. The great failure of the university is that they don't explain to the legislature, to the parents of young people, what they really want. What they really want is to participate in the old vision of the university as a place of leisure where people learn how to make something of their lives, not a rat race where you're cramming information into students as fast as you can. This vision is what the lower classes thought that these people in the Ivy League were enjoying and this is what they wanted something of, but by the time they get there, the university's been turned into kind of a General Motors that has very little resemblance to what they thought they were going to get if they could just get their kid into the university, and this can be explained to legislatures. I've had the experience of discovering that they have been insulted by academic people who come to them for money and assume that the legislators were men without any vision or human understanding at all, that all they understood is bread-and-butter and building up our industry and stuff like that. The man who goes to them and tells them about why it is essential that we have philosophy taught at this university, they'll appreciate that very much, and will give more money to the philosophy department than it would get by somehow trying to hitch itself on to building our national power.

KATZ: I want to ask my two colleagues how are we going to get there? How are we going to get these kinds of institutions?

SANFORD: The question naturally comes out concerning a new institution such as ours, what are we trying to do, are we trying to build a model which we hope somebody will eventually imitate, or are we trying to somehow influence the university next door by more active types of intervention, and that's a very hard question. For example, in a way, we are a new model for training in clinical psychology. Well, what are we going to do, set up a whole aggregate of such institutions around the country? That's one idea. We've been under great pressure to set up Wright Institute graduate training programs in Washington, L.A., Chicago, and so on, and be a national university, organized along the same principle.

HALLECK: One way we could get there politically would be to attack the whole grant system. I think it's one of the biggest corruptions.

SANFORD: That's ruined undergraduate education more than anything.

KATZ: Well, I doubt that the faculty will do it. I doubt that the legislators will do it. I think the only hope is the pressure that will come from students. That's a very slim hope at the moment.

SANFORD: That's the big point. The pressure is coming from the grass roots you see. I'm strong on getting more women into the system, not for the reasons women are, but because I think this is a great hope for changing the system, and that's one of the big points about our graduate school. Half of our students are women, and we are truly democratic in the sense that everybody really participates in all the decisions affecting him and her. We are bound to have a different kind of community and a different kind of education than you get elsewhere. Similarly for the Blacks. It's fundamental, I think, that if you really want to shake up a university, even a big one, admit all at once, 500 or 1000 Black students, and the thing will just change, because they will immediately attack the institutional racism that has persisted there, because they know damn well that it's not that individuals don't like Blacks that gets in their way, it's that we've built up a system that simply cannot accommodate itself to the needs of Black people, and so something has to give. And the kinds of change that the presence of a lot of Third World people require are precisely those which I would insist upon the basis of what I would consider good educational policy.

BLOOM: Now, like a good symphony, I want to recapitulate the first theme at the end and allow you a chance to make whatever concluding remarks you want to on the general subject that we started out with, the issue of stress on the campus. I'd be pleased if you would use our last few moments to say whatever you want to say that seems most important to you at this time.

SANFORD: Instead of trying to diagnose this generation of students, diagnose the particular pattern of stress exhibited by some students, and put the emphasis on using such knowledge as we already have to build the right kinds of institutions for the future. Now, it's true that it's very hard to start out within an institution and change it in that direction. The only device I have thought of that had any chance at all of being effective is the approach of interviewing faculty in depth and then bringing the results into open discussion with the faculty. That has great potency. But meanwhile, it's a very stimulating and challenging and exciting thing to think about the future with special reference to the kinds of institutions and communities that we can build, given such knowledge as we have. What we've got in our graduate school are things which psychologists have been saying for years are true and beautiful, only they've never put them in their own departments. As Carl Rogers has pointed out, psychologists in all their teaching ignore all of their own most dearly held principles.

KATZ: I agree there's a lot of knowledge to build on. One of the problems is that that knowledge is not widely shared. I'm impressed by how little faculty, or administrators, or even student personnel people often know about students. To my mind it is terribly important to increase our listening to students and to expend much more effort to find out about them; particularly these days, when there are almost constant changes. I do not see it as a passive listening, but as part of an interaction in which students can become partners in designing the institution in all its aspects: the residences, the academic program, and so on. If I had to single out just one particular thing, I would say that listening and interacting is a precondition to almost everything else that we have said here.

HALLECK: I'm not too optimistic that the grassroots movement is what will bring about the changes we have been talking about. I don't think you can leave it to the kids. There has to be some impetus coming from the faculty as well.

INDEX

278

279

help-seeking, 125-152
married, 219-229
See also Dropouts; Mental
health
Subgroups, 32-33, 35
Summerskill, J., 99, 102, 104
Superego system, 64
Sydney, University of, 168

Taiwan, campus mental health
in, 168
Telephone counseling service,
202, 231-243
Tenure, 265
Texas, University of, at Austin,
234
Thurlow, H. J., 127, 139-145,
147-149
Timmons, Frank R., 99-119
Transactional Analysis of Per-
sonality-Environment (TAPE),
31, 32, 35, 37, 109-110
Trent, J. W., 106
Twain, Mark, 48
Tyler, Mary, 231-243

Uganda, campus mental health
in, 167
University College, London, 161
Uppsala, University of, 165, 172

Vali-Wohl, A., 164, 172
Value conflict, 29
van de Voorde, H., 165
Vauhkonen, K., 166

Walters, O. S., 127, 139, 142,
143, 145
Wedge, B. M., 154

Weiss, R. J., 126, 135, 155
West, M., 127, 135
West Germany, campus mental
health in, 164
Western Interstate Commission
for Higher Education
(WICHE), 197, 198, 215
Western Ontario, University of,
127
Western Regional Education
Compact, 197
White, R. W., 51
Whittington, H. G., 154
Wilkie, G. H., 153
Windham, Thomas L., 77-86
Wisconsin, University of, 103,
127
Women, 248-249, 275
occupational development, 59,
61
sexual development, 54
World Federation for Mental
Health (WFMH), 158, 159
World Health Organization
(WHO), 157-160
World Union of Organizations
for the Safeguard of
Youth, 156
World University Service,
157, 169
Wright Institute, 272-274
Wright-Short, F. W., 156, 168,
171

Yale University, 28, 126
Yalom, I. D., 193
Yeh, E.-k., 156, 168

Ziolko, H.-U., 157, 164, 175